Zen: A Dog's Tale

The Race to Alaska

Robert McCall

ISBN: 978-1-7393510-0-7

For Uncle Pete.

Look what you started...

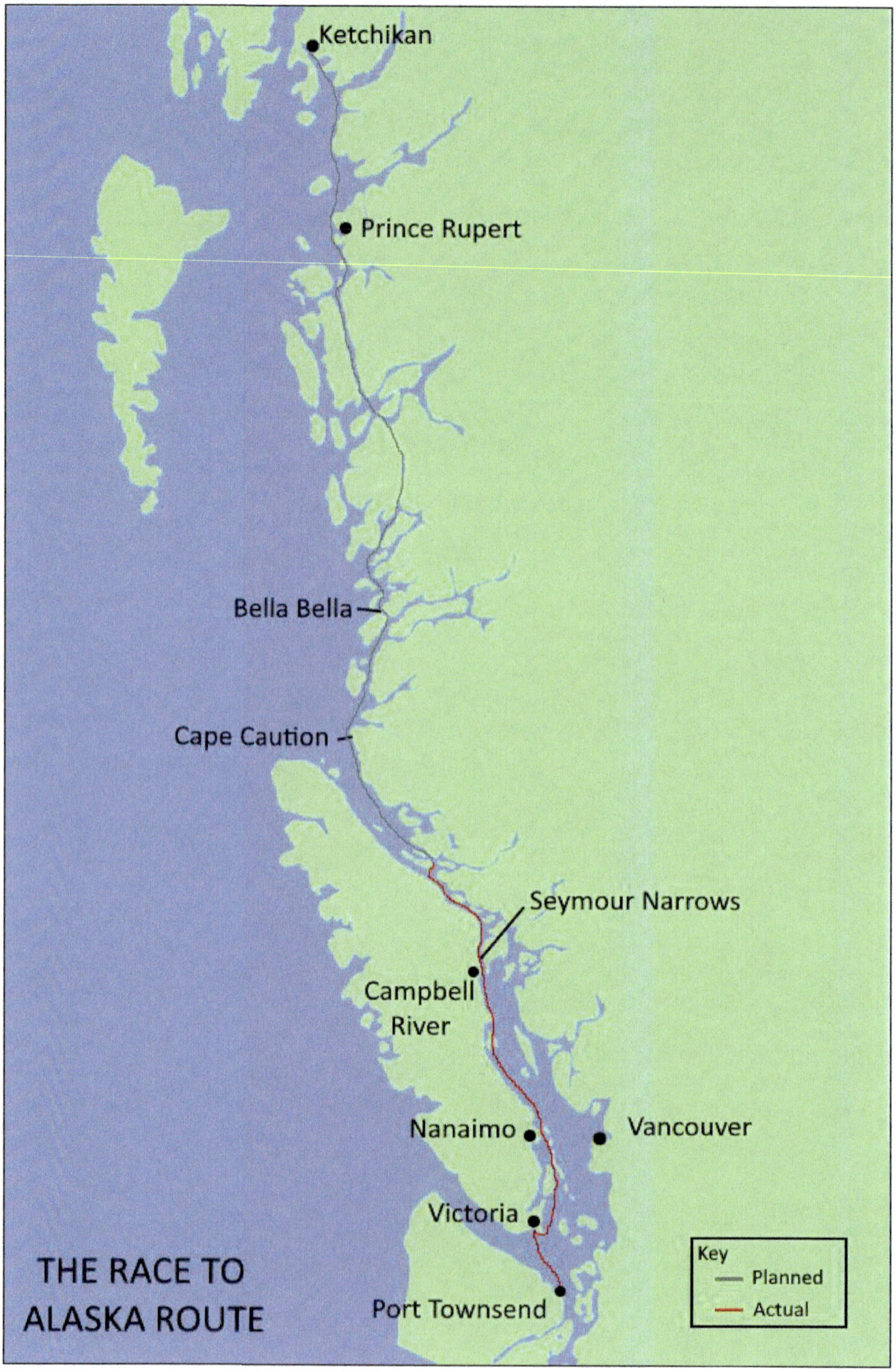
Ketchikan
Prince Rupert
Bella Bella
Cape Caution
Seymour Narrows
Campbell River
Nanaimo
Vancouver
Victoria
Port Townsend
THE RACE TO ALASKA ROUTE
Key
Planned
Actual

Contents

Preparation

2014 to 2017.

Because it is there.

All it takes is the germ of an idea to infect your imagination, and, more often than not, you'll catch those germs from your mates. Darran Williams had become an acquaintance of mine through a shared obsession with the Yukon River Quest (YRQ), a four-hundred-and-forty-four-mile descent of the Yukon River in North-West Canada. We'd met the previous year in Norwich, and he'd gleefully shared his racing experiences, and plenty of tips and tricks for inland expedition racing. These experiences came from his chaotic first attempt, where he'd finished almost stone cold last through sheer lack of planning preparation, and no small quantity of stubbornness. These were backed up by a more rigorous regime to return the following year, which delivered him a second-place finish. So, he'd already completed the race twice, and I was limbering up for it in August 2014, when he shared a video clip of a new event he'd found online.

I can clearly remember watching it in the office that lunchtime. The short film showed a guy fly from Port Townsend in Washington State, up to a beach in Alaska, nail ten thousand dollars to a tree, and sound a starting hooter to throw down the first ever challenge to sail, row, or paddle seven hundred and fifty miles to Alaska. There were only two stipulations laid down in the film: no engines were allowed, and no support.

I can also clearly remember my reaction to watching it. I immediately forwarded the video to my colleague, Mike. In addition to telling him that he had to take a look at it, and saying that it was pretty nuts, I also said to Mike "I could never do that." At that moment in time, this was true. I was an inland racer. The only races I had taken part in of note were the Devizes to Westminster Canoe Race, a one hundred and twenty-five mile yomp down the Thames, and the Cheshire Ring Canoe Race. I was absorbed in planning for my first attempt at the Yukon River Quest, which even as an inland race was taking over all my free time. Race to Alaska was a seagoing race. I knew precious little about the sea, except that in a kayak it could be bloody dangerous. I knew about the Lyme Bay disaster from the nineties, which had claimed the lives of four teenagers and gave me a respectful fear of open water. I also knew that paddling alone in a boat, even in a two-man kayak, was out there, extreme, even foolhardy. However, as click-bait for an event went, it caught my attention.

At that moment, and for quite a while after, the Race to Alaska wasn't for me. I had other targets. I'd been obsessing over the Yukon River Quest since 2011, and I knew this seagoing venture was beyond me, but the germ of interest in the event was there. I Googled the course. This didn't really dampen my view of its feasibility. The first leg of the race crossed from the Washington State mainland – Olympia – to Victoria on Vancouver Island. It looked... big. Then looking further North beyond Vancouver Island there was a big expanse of Pacific, and, well... it was the Pacific. Not a lake, a bay, or even a sea, but a bloody ocean! There was this big expanse of exposed coast with a place called Cape Caution smack bang in the middle of it. Then there were loads of islands, and what looked like potential routes through them. I recall thinking that the beginning was scary, and the second half was pretty damn intimidating, but at least for the best part of three hundred miles the bit behind Vancouver Island was sheltered and would be more straightforward. That assumption would expose itself for the naivety it was founded on very soon...

The first ever Race to Alaska, or R2AK, was set for June 2015, and I signed on for race notifications. One of the big draws that made it attractive to an observer was the turn of phrase in the writeups describing what it was all about.

> *"This isn't for everyone. It's like the Iditarod, on a boat, with a chance of drowning, being run down by a freighter, or eaten by a grizzly bear. There are squalls, killer whales, tidal currents that run upwards of 20 miles an hour, and some of the most beautiful scenery on earth". (R2AK website)*

It was scaring the blades off your paddles, and at the same time enticing you to follow it. When that race came around in 2015, I was resolved to follow it.

What unfolded over the next few weeks that June was utterly spellbinding. I can vividly remember sitting watching the tracker as Elsie Piddock pipped MOB Mentality to the finish line. Given I was a kayaking enthusiast following a sailing race, that in itself was a transformation, a broadening of horizons. But the genius in the event was the drama that unfolded all the way through the field across all the craft. I have no idea if Jake Beattie, the Washington State wacko who came up with the concept of the race, expected the drama of a first stage that challenged the smaller craft to make the cut-off deadline in Victoria, or the carnage that a storm wreaked on the third day of the race proper, but it was enthralling. There was the genius of Roger Mann, sailing his Hobie through crazy conditions in Johnstone Strait, munching his way through four Big Macs in Campbell River to keep the calorie count sufficiently high to complete the race in twelve days. And then there was Mike, of Team Mike's Kayak who, averaging thirty miles a day, did it for the little guy and proved that it *was* possible to nail the race in a nineteen-foot piece of fibreglass.

The real draw came from the write-ups posted every day – the R2AK Daily Updates – by the race organisers. These are at the core of each race, and the turn of phrase to communicate the successes, calamities, overcoming of adversity, and the plain mundane of expedition racing just epitomises everything that is genius about the event. The identity of the author of these blogs is a closely guarded secret, but I suspect that either Daniel Evans or Jake Beattie would be present in the identification parade were suspects to be singled out. Here was a race that is devoid of the gamesmanship of major league competition, imbued with the camaraderie and sportsmanship that resonated with my idea of what sport should be. Jake himself describes the race as the antidote to the America's Cup, where big money is king and sporting prowess is eclipsed by technology. My fascination with the race stemmed from what crews did to overcome the limits of not having an engine (in the case of the sailboats), and in the pure brazenness in the face of overwhelming conditions and distance for the really little guys, in particular the rowers, and especially the kayakers.

I was hooked. The germ of an idea from back in 2014 had now grown into a proper triffid of thoughts. I was also more enlightened after the storms that hit the race in Georgia Strait, and now being fully aware of the challenges of Seymour Narrows, that the Inside Passage behind Vancouver Island was to be feared and respected just as much as Juan de Fuca, Cape Caution, and the rest of the course. But I was also starting to think in a different way, not yet at the point of overturning my initial reaction to be able to participate, but in terms of how crews were solving problems. By the time the 2016 race started, I was locked in, much in the same way that the organisers had established the formula for daily updates, clips of the day, and had promoted the race tracker.

2016 was Mad Dog's year, but behind there were stories to take note of. The Wabi Sabi close encounters of the ursine kind, combined with poo story – no race is really complete without a poo story – brough home the real grizzly risks. There were small boats, even an SUP, but not so many little guys that year. Mathieu Bonnier in his Liteboat was the nearest beyond Karl to a human-powered boat, but he still had a sail. 2016 was definitely a sailor's race, and I was inwardly hoping that it didn't turn all Sydney to Hobart over the coming years.

2017 : Yukon

We choose... to do the other things. Not because they are easy, but because they are hard.

By the time I lined up for the Yukon River Quest in 2017, following the R2AK had become an annual must-follow event for me. I remember sitting in my hotel room in Whitehorse the night before starting that race, reading the Day 15 write-up about Karl Kruger's race that year – "A dance about architecture". To say Karl is a legend is an understatement. He was the guy who made the first attempt at the R2AK in the human powered category on a stand-up paddleboard in 2016, only to have the board break under him. Undeterred, and sure of his ability to finish, he'd returned, and not only finished the race, but in the process set the record for the fastest ever human-powered entry. It was staggering. Watching the video where he discussed what he'd achieved after the race, and just after I had finished mine, was inspiring. I cannot hold a candle to Karl and his abilities, but it dismissed more reasons why this race was not impossible, just that it was bloody, bloody hard.

It wasn't just Karl's achievement that was flipping switches. The Yukon River Quest that year really changed the balance for me. The previous year's attempt at the YRQ had ended prematurely in Carmacks, only one hundred and fifty miles into the race, way short of the finish, and I considered it a failure, and it bloody hurt. That hurt stemmed from a feeling that, had we even taken a thirty-minute nap, we may have been able to have complete the course. Whether that was justified or not, I was carrying the wounds for that DNF, and they cut deep. The return – solo – in 2017 not only healed those wounds, but also gave me a sense of what is achievable. Then again, it gave me far more than that...

I have been competing in events most of my life. We like to joke, my friends and I, that I don't have a competitive bone in my body. And I'll admit this is about as far from how I am as could be. I would like to think that I don't compete against others (although some may disagree); positions in races mean little to me, but I have always competed against myself, benchmark times, and against the challenge of finishing, to be the best I can be, and in this I am uber, uber driven. It also meant that, prior to the 2017 YRQ, I was more often than not focussed on crossing the finish line. I can vividly recall all my attention running the 2007 London Marathon focused on my watch, calculating the time I was likely to finish the race in, and I could tell you virtually nothing about the course from mile 21, save the demotivation of being overtaken by blokes dressed respectively as Elvis and a caveman. The focus, on turning up for Yukon River Quest, was therefore myopically set on getting over the finish line.

That competitive ethos took a huge smack in the chops thirty-six hours in. It was closing in on midnight and we were nearing Five Finger Rapids, almost the only section of white water on the course. At this point, I was pretty wired through lack of sleep. I had been up for over forty hours, and I was paddling with three other participants. We had a sort of tacit agreement that we were paddling as a group. We rounded a bend in the river to see the most jaw-dropping sight of the sun, the midnight sun, kissing the top of the ridge in front of us. My jaw hit the deck of the boat. The water was glistening gold in its light, and this then extended to the rocky outcrops on the bank similarly glowing gold in the sun's midnight light, save where the rocks sharply shadowed to absolute black. It flipped the biggest switch of them all in my head. In that instant, my mindset went from "I want to finish this damn race" to "Right now, there is nowhere else in this world that I would rather be". I don't think I would have experienced it in the same way if I hadn't also been feeling the effects of sleep deprivation or the extreme fatigue and pain my body was undergoing, but for me it was a metaphorical drinking from the cup. I felt like I entered a strange state of pain-induced bliss.

Midnight sun at Five Finger Rapids in the Yukon

Surfers go surfing in search of the ultimate ride, and while I am not clear in my head that this was what I was searching for, I'd accidentally found that piece of perfection, a feeling of serene contentment, in an entirely different way, one that did not last for a few seconds, but for the entire remainder of the Yukon River Quest. Furthermore, the best of the feeling was not only knowing at the time that what I was experiencing was very, very special, but also that it stayed with me for long after the race finished, and it still does. I have experienced that moment of a lifetime, where everything aligns, and whether I experience it again or not, nothing can take that away from me. Taking part in events took on a different dimension from that moment, and I began to appreciate where I was more than to think about where I was headed.

Finishing with the group of three other paddlers, Marieke, Sergey, and Wolfgang, also gave me thought for how it was possible to compete safely in the Race to Alaska. I think, up until that point, my thoughts had been to rope in someone else to race in a two-man sea kayak (insofar as I was thinking about taking part at all). Racing with three other solos gave rise to a new perspective: if you paddle in a group of three boats, there are benefits. Firstly, there is safety in having other boats in the vicinity, so if you capsize there's someone else to come help you. Secondly, you are not stuck within two metres of the other person for the duration of the race. You could counter this line of reasoning by saying "find the right partner", but I'm not levelling this at other people, I'm levelling it at me. I am not the easiest person to get on with in a boat, and I can be an absolute sod when interpersonal things start going wrong. My thoughts on this were that, having a group of three would cover the safety aspects of sea kayaking, while allowing each person to paddle at a distance if they were (I was) being cranky and not have to completely get on. This rationale then led me on to thinking about who would make suitable candidates for "the other two".

All of this, Karl's achievements, and my own lesser redemptions in the Yukon, still hadn't got me to a point where I was committing to the Race to Alaska as my next big project. However, clearly by now the barriers to it were crumbling rapidly. There were still some major issues which were potential showstoppers for taking part. Not least was my own competence when it came to sea kayaking. While my inland marathon paddling experience was extensive, albeit at a mediocre level, my sea paddling abilities were virtually non-existent. I could count on the fingers of one hand how many times I'd paddled on the sea: I had kayaked around a small island off Porquerolles in the South of France in a general-purpose boat as a teenager, a markedly stupid thing to have done given the size of the waves we paddled in and the lack of buoyancy in the boats. I had been kayak-surfing at Sheringham in Norfolk for a weekend where, believe me, the height of the surf wouldn't frighten a flounder. Then again, still in my teens, I'd been on a trip to the best surfing beach in Wales at Rhossili Bay, yet again in a general-purpose kayak, only to find the conditions there as flat as a pancake. The only proper sea kayaking I had done was on two trips to Port McNeill on Vancouver Island, once on honeymoon in my early twenties, and more recently in 2015 as a family holiday, where we had wilderness paddled in guided groups for a week each time. While the experience of these trips was motivational in wanting to take part in R2AK, both were under the control of someone who knew what they were doing, and both in almost ideal conditions.

I'd read plenty over the years about what it takes to paddle on the sea, and I wasn't that much of a plonker that I didn't know that I was lacking not only the experience of sea paddling, but also the skill set to make it safe. In my head these boiled down into several significant abilities.

Firstly, and most obviously, I'd need to be experienced in sea kayaking. I'd need to know how to self-rescue, how to land a kayak in surf and be able to set off again, and although I could roll, I'd need to have a bomb-proof way of making sure that I could handle myself back upright, alone. I'd need to know how to navigate, which not only included being able to read a nautical chart and set a hazard-free route, but also how to plan for tidal changes. This would have to be complemented with knowledge of how to use weather data, and be able to read that data, both from weather maps, and also from clouds and the water. For safety's sake, I would need to be able to use a short-wave radio, and also know how to repair whatever kayak I was paddling in for the race. These were the headline requirements, all significantly lacking from my repertoire, and these didn't even touch on the wilderness skills or local knowledge I would need to take part.

2018 : Two steps forward, one step back.

The greater our knowledge increases, the greater our ignorance unfolds.

This may sound to you like I'd committed to my next project, but I think honestly at this time I was not there yet, and there were clouds gathering which required a different set of navigational skills. We were now in 2018, and the full impact of the post YRQ hangover had hit and hit hard. When you achieve a goal, you can only feed off its success for a while before the taste goes stale. I trained hard that winter with my friend Gaz for the Devizes to Westminster, but we were foiled by flooding on the Thames which curtailed the race. We didn't even start the shortened version, which I'll freely admit was my decision. It felt like we had wasted all of the training sessions we had so fastidiously completed in the cold, dark and wet, six days a week, for over three months.

Pulling that rug from underneath us denied us both the sense of achievement that comes with a big race, and I think ultimately it led to the demise of our racing partnership, although Gaz subsequently suffering from frozen shoulder for twelve months also contributed. It wasn't the only cowpat I was rolling through that year. Work was not going well. The team at work I belonged to, a group of around fifteen, was now living with the very real threat of being outsourced from the company I'd been working at for nearly twenty years. As I watched work projects I'd expected lead, or at least to be part of, go to people in the "in crowd", I was also feeling the double whammy of being actively not wanted and excluded from the progression route I was expecting to take. It didn't help that the working relations I had with my team lead, and far worse the senior manager overseeing the department, were close to rock bottom. In Jane, I was also beginning to lose a paddle partner I'd had for eight years, and whom I'd taken for granted would always be there to train with. She'd rediscovered cycling, and between work, cycling and paddling, something had to give, and that was paddling. It wasn't handled well. With everything else going on, this felt like a betrayal of our paddling partnership, and I took it very badly. For me, work and sport are two strands in life that are hugely important to my well-being and having all of this misfiring in 2018 was impacting me acutely.

Away from paddling, I was trying to plan a long game that would mitigate the inevitable outsource at work and provide a means to resolve my situation there. That plan involved going back to university, which began to occupy some of my spare time and encroached a little on planning time. As a dream, though, R2AK was also beginning to form part of that long game, and for that I'd been thinking a lot about the experience of paddling in that group in Yukon. It seemed a logical step to find like-minded loons who would be interested in joining me in that group of three. Three was the magic number, certainly no more than that. Sergey from that group was the logical ideal candidate, but when I asked, he replied that finding the time, holiday time, for that length of venture would be impossible. The next person on the list was Marieke.

Marieke took some very careful consideration. In the Yukon race, on the last night, things had not gone exactly swimmingly between the pair of us. I put this down to a level of psychosis on both our parts, attributable to extreme sleep deprivation, physical fatigue, and the consumption of copious quantities of caffeine tablets. On the last night of the race, we had nearly come to blows over the approach to river navigation, and at one point the group nearly split into two over the stop/start effects of those navigational tactics we were employing. I am not going to lay all of this at her door either, because I really am difficult when things are not going the way I would like them to, and I was carrying a torn bicep which was making me grumpier than Victor Meldrew at a drive-in scrapyard. Furthermore, at the end of the race, she'd had the perfidy to make a break from the group and finish ahead of the three of us, something that didn't entirely fit with the sporting ethos I had expected. However, she had saved my race not once, but twice. On the first night she'd administered anti-sickness tablets which allowed me to keep the calories coming in, and then on the third day, she'd dug out a Paracetamol/ Ibuprofen cocktail which had deadened the pain from the bicep tear and allowed me to carry on paddling, and ultimately to get to the finish.

We weren't exactly buddies at this point either. After the Yukon race, there's a presentation, where all the competitors gather for a dinner and sit together. The three of us, Wolfgang, Sergey, and myself sat at one table, Marieke with a different bunch of mates at another. That evening, I went for dinner with another friend from the race, Steve Morrison, and bumped into Marieke in the restaurant. As Steve had not yet arrived, I joined her and her friends for a beer while I waited. The conversation came within a whisker of degenerating into a blame game for the things that went wrong in the race, and I think both of us had to make a conscious effort to pull it back to something more civil. Importantly though, we had exchanged contact details, and we were still in touch. She'd written a piece on her Yukon experience, as had I, and it had been an interesting exercise to compare those. As she said, we could have been paddling separate events, such was the disparity between our recollections.

The more I thought about Marieke, and the more we talked about things over email and text – not about Alaska, but about racing in general – the more I thought she had the potential to be a racing partner, but I was already adamant in my mind that paddling in separate boats was non-negotiable. I knew deep down there would be moments where we didn't get on. I think it was June when I put the race to her. I can remember being sat in the Saffron Lane Athletics Stadium in Leicester on a video call, discussing the possibility of teaming up. We went over the ups and the downs of the Yukon race and discussed (maybe naively at the time) what paddling to Alaska would require. It was a frank, open discussion of what we'd not done well in Canada, and what we could do to overcome the interpersonal issues we had and could again face on a bigger trip. It was a really upbeat, positive conversation, and by the end of it we had a more than tentative agreement at a partnership. I now had a year in mind to race. 2020 fit the bill. There was probably enough time to prepare to go out and race, and I would be fifty. It felt like a birthday present to myself to be able to go do it then. Now we were looking for a third person to make the team. It wasn't a full commitment to the race, but the idea of it being impossible had gone. I was now looking at a series of challenges to get to the start line.

The first of these was, unsurprisingly, sea kayaking. I signed myself up for a weekend course up in Anglesey with Roger Chandler of Coastal Spirit that August. I packed some of my older gear, including a wetsuit I'd had for about twenty years, and headed up to Holyhead for that weekend. The course I'd signed up for was British Canoeing's then three-star qualification. I had it in my mind this was a good point to pitch in at, as I had plenty of technique from paddling white water in my teens. I also decided to take the approach that I knew nothing about the sea, which was a fair one to take, as I didn't, and I tried to leave any arrogance and misplaced overconfidence in ability at the door. I had no idea if I was overreaching myself with the three stars, but I was pretty certain that someone like Roger would put me in my place pretty sharpish.

It was glorious sunshine when I arrived at the Anglesey Outdoors Centre. Roger turned up in his transit on the Saturday morning, and we selected what would be a suitable boat to go paddle in. He kitted me out with the necessary peripheral kit, spray deck, towline, pump, and paddles – I only had wing paddles, and fully expected to need to be using blades more suited to the sea. When we reached the beach with the other two course participants, I donned my wetsuit. Having not worn it for over a decade, this was a bit of a problem. Middle aged spread and a change in body shape from paddling meant it was a very tight fit. I managed to get it on, but it was pulling on my shoulders and movement was somewhat restricted.

Roger told me afterwards that his first opinions of my paddling were close to "Oh my god". I was right to have left the thoughts that I had the ability at the door. I was atrocious. He started me with low brace turns in the bay, and immediately exposed technical deficiencies in what I was doing. Brace too far back, not looking sideways at where I was bracing, not a clue how to use my knees and feet to enhance the turns. I'd like to think I listened. I tried to be as receptive as possible to his advice. It was requiring a lot of concentration on my part, and I was making a lot of mistakes, but I was learning, and above all it was fun!

Learning the basics. Anglesey with Coastal Spirit. Courtesy of Roger Chandler

Before we left the bay Roger got me to roll the boat. I handed him my hat and glasses, and pulled off one of the clumsiest, flukiest rolls of my life. I came back up, but far more by luck than skill. Over the course of the rest of the weekend, I was to try numerous more times to roll outside of the bays, and I was to fail on each occasion. Something that had been natural to me as a kid was lost. The to-learn list, or in this case re-learn list, was getting longer. The rest of the course was fantastic. I have a great deal of respect for Roger and the way he teaches. There was never a negative moment in the way he communicated what needed to be learned. There were exercises, like the all-in rescue, where he asked us as a group to figure out the approach, and it often felt more like a jolly on the water rather than a course. I knew then that I'd be going back to Roger repeatedly for coaching and advice. By the end of the weekend, I was beginning to accommodate the techniques he was imparting, and I was hitting the levels that the three-star required. The only downside was damage that I was causing to my shoulder from the tightness of the wetsuit: the pressure it was exerting caused a great deal of discomfort. I had drysuit envy for the other guys, and there was now another item at least on the kit list.

After the weekend's sessions had finished, Roger and I sat down at the Paddler's Rest for a beer and a chat. I explained to him about the Race to Alaska, and what I wanted to achieve. To his credit, Roger didn't shoot me down. I was looking for a mentor, I guess, and in Roger found someone I felt I could come back to if I needed advice. I was to return for several more weekends with Roger after that, and I'm grateful for all of the guidance I have had from him.

That August also gave me a different insight into expedition ideas when I attended the Adventure Film Festival in Mill Hill, London. This was a film festival run by a motorbike enthusiast who broadened the film horizon to cover anything left-field and interesting, and above all created with a "home-made" ethos. It wasn't the films that triggered the thought process, but a sideshow demonstration by a couple of guys who had done a trip through the Amazon. As tents were rather susceptible to the plethora of creepy-crawlies there, they'd taken hammocks to camp in. The demo not only described the process of setting up different types of hammocks with tarpaulins over the top to keep the rain out, but also let us try them out. In my ignorance, I'd always assumed that you slept on your back in a hammock, curved to its shape and unable to move. It was a revelation to find that you could sleep on your side, and that the hammock shapes itself to you. Hammocks went on the "to experiment with" list.

The next piece of the puzzle to find and fit was a boat. I had racing kayaks, and a general-purpose boat, but not a sea kayak. Other than the trips to Vancouver Island, I'd never really paddled a sea kayak, and paddling there was of the two-man variety, not solo. Even the trip to the Yukon had involved a marathon/sea hybrid in the form of an Epic Endurance. While I was in Anglesey, there were Rockpool kayaks to go try out. I had visited Mike, the man behind Rockpool, at his workshop and managed to borrow a Rockpool Taran for a day to go and try out in the bay. It was an eye-opening experience. Compared to what I was expecting of a touring sea kayak, this was a remarkably unstable boat. I felt I was near the limits of my comfort zone even in the bay, and not out in the more exposed sea. It was, no doubt, a beautiful boat, but not for me.

It was back home, and in September, that I spotted a Valley Aquanaut for sale in one for the "For Sale and Wanted" groups on Facebook. It was a second-hand boat, and a very reasonable price for a sea kayak, and apparently in good condition. To cap it all, the guy selling it lived all of half an hour from me. I organised a try-out over on the Avon, a stretch of river I had no familiarity with. It was a lovely craft, with a blue deck, white hull, and clearly well maintained. In the short spin I took it on I tried another roll, which came off impeccably. While it might not be the boat I would end up racing in, it was clearly more than suitable for all of the training I would have to do.

So, I now had a boat, and so over in Holland did Marieke. She had acquired an Epic surfski to train on. Having a team mate on board was also beginning to shape and motivate the planning process for the race. This involved identifying our skills gaps, a lot of kit searches, discussions on sponsorship, and trying to figure out what we would need to do to qualify for the race. It was around this time I contacted the race organisers to sound out our suitability for taking part:

Email to the R2AK team, dated October 14, 2018:

> *I've followed the race since you nailed that wonga to a tree in 2014. I'm a kayaker. I mainly do inland endurance races. in 2014 I thought R2AK was beyond me, but a lot has happened since then, and I think different now, so...*
>
> *The plan:*
>
> *I wanna race in 2020. No. I'm gonna race in 2020. Actually, it's "We". We're gonna race in 2020. Note: 2020. In K1's, we will be three, as three is the magic number, and it's so much more fun in a group than on your lonesome.*
>
> *This is a declaration of intent. We are not ready. Yet. But we will be.*
>
> *So.... I wanted to start a dialog with you now, hence this. I am happy to start the vetting process for 2020, if you think that is appropriate. But mostly I just wanted to say... "We're coming."*
>
> *Hat. Ring. Done.*

The reply that came back from Daniel fit the R2AK bill:

> *Let me be the first (or second? twentieth?) to tell how bad an idea that is. In the best occasion racing engineless to Alaska is not the brightest notion. Did you say K1? Sadly, the words knuckleheaded and adventurous are twinned to the same ancestry.*
>
> *Well, me and the team will be here in 2020 as long as the creek don't rise. And we'll vet you then. It doesn't sound impossible though. Is that what you were looking for? I'm holding onto your hat. It's a good one.*

None of us were to realise how far that creek would rise at this stage!

That the emails reflected the daily updates on the websites, but in a not-discouraging way, was heartening. We carried on our search for a third but over the next couple of months, I think we both separately reached the conclusion that we would be a two. I felt I was never going to find someone who balanced us, and that neither would Marieke. Quietly, we settled to plan as a pair.

2019 : Rebuilding

As 2018 drew to a close, I was physically in deep trouble. The problem that had begun with that tight wetsuit in Anglesey had morphed into a full-on issue. I had to stop paddling through the pain in what I thought was my right arm. After years of intense training this had a knock-on effect into my sleeping patterns. I was crashing out at ten or eleven, only to wake up at one and not be able to go back to sleep again. With the non-paddling issues of 2018, this was tearing me apart, and I hit a huge low for the last three months of the year. By the time I hit New Year's Eve, I was trying to force the sleep with tablets from the pharmacist, but I was waking up in a chemical haze still in the middle of the night, and the pain was seeping through, no doubt the cause of my unwanted consciousness. That New Year's Eve morning was the last straw. I sought an emergency appointment with my GP and started a protracted and laborious process of check-ups and scans. By February I had the results: I had two tears in my shoulder, bursitis (the inflammation of a fluid sac under the joint) causing a not inconsiderable amount of pain, and to cap it off, the beginnings of arthritis in the shoulder joint.

While the medical diagnosis was underway, I took action to attempt to fix things. Gaz recommended a podiatrist friend in Tamworth, Leon, who began a series of treatment which were to last about six months. These involved electrocuting my shoulder with an industrial strength TENS machine, the logic being that it broke down the scar tissue and encouraged blood to flow into the shocked area. It was the most bizarre of feelings, taking as much electrical current as my pain threshold would allow, and watching my arm elevate itself with no intent from me, so that the upper arm was horizontally aligned to my shoulder. To begin with, I had two sessions a week with Leon, then once a fortnight, and eventually once a month as it subsided. I felt a million bucks leaving his practice in the evenings, but the following day would be back to pain, albeit lesser each time. Leon also put me on to using a TENS machine away from the sessions to back up the treatment.

Having begun treatment with Leon, and under his guidance, I also started back in the boat, the boat being the Aquanaut. It had had virtually no use since I'd bought it the previous autumn. The first paddle was a ten-minute jaunt from my usual paddling base of Basinbridge Lane. It hurt like stink, but it was mentally great to be back on the water. The sessions gradually built, mile by mile until I was paddling something close to what I could mentally accept as a training session. I wasn't feeling completely right, but I was headed in the right direction.

I also started to try and contact previous R2AK paddlers. In my mind, the prime candidate for contact was Mike, of Team Mike's Kayak from the first race. I'd found out a lot about his race from the Inside Passage Registry, an extensive online resource which included write-ups of trips completed, including Mike's. Beyond this, I knew very little about him, save his name, and that he was from California. I emailed my Yukon friends in California, with the daftest of questions: "I'm looking for Mike Higgins, from California, who paddled the R2AK in 2015. Do you know him?" It was nearly as bad as being asked if you knew John Smith from London. "Sure", came the reply, along with Mike's email address. Now we had two lines into the R2AK community. I emailed Mike with a bunch of questions, the first of which was about the maps that he had used to navigate the course. I expected a response detailing some specialist or niche cartography, but what I got was more leftfield: "I had terrible maps, just printouts from Google Maps that were almost high enough resolution to navigate by."

In March I enrolled on two courses at Kingston Canoe Club with Howard Jeffs, the first in boat repair, amusingly titled "Smash and Bash", and the second the following day in navigation. The venue was in the club centre under Kingston Bridge arches, and it was bloody cold, which wasn't so bad for the first day, but for sitting still through the navigation course on the second day, a bit of a trial. The smash and bash course was brilliant. There was something intensely gratifying about taking an ice axe to an old kayak, puncturing a hole right through the hull, and being able to apply a full fibreglass fix to the inflicted damage. While I could never profess to be proficient at boat repairs, I now had a feeling that I could at least make a valiant attempt at a fix should the need arise.

The navigation course was a different beast, not because the course was bad, but because there was just so much to take in from my inadequate starting point. Combined with the arctic temperatures under the arches, I was trying to get to grips with tide charts, current maps, weather information, compass bearings… the lot. I came out feeling I'd just filled a bookshelf in my mind with a whole load of new reading material but failed to absorb any of the contents.

As Easter approached, I had my annual commitment to the Devizes to Westminster Canoe Race, but unlike previous years, and for the first time ever, not in a competitive capacity. It was a tough gig mentally to not be on the water, but there was no way I was fit enough to participate properly.

Two friends from the States were taking part. I had met Holly Crouch at the Yukon in 2017, and Nicholas Goulden was an ex-pat friend of several other Yukoners, Elaine, Tom, and Emily. I had also committed to providing support on the tideway to two other great friends, Natasha and Max Kimberley, who were going for the more niche achievement of being the first high kneeling two-man crew to complete the course, and a mother-son crew at that. I do bear a fair bit of responsibility for having helped talk them into attempting it, although in all honesty it didn't take much persuasion.

It was a brilliant weekend, although I think I made a lousy pit crew member. After a Good Friday stalking Nicholas on the four-day race, and at the last minute, I rather randomly teamed up with Rachel Dennis, the race volunteer co-ordinator. We followed Holly and her partner down to Westminster, occasionally managing to help them en route, and only once being told (not by Holly) to fuck off. It was a hoot, although we kept bumping into people we knew and missing Holly as she passed by. I spent the last night in Teddington trying out the hammock before following the Kimberleys down the tideway in the Aquanaut. It was the longest paddle I'd managed that year, and my shoulder really felt like it was heading in the right direction. Watching a high kneeler canoe paddled well is a thing to be marvelled at, especially in a glorious dawn on the Thames Tideway. These two loons were making something that many would consider impossible look not only straightforward, but graceful – much like Karl on his paddleboard.

In the aftermath of the race, I agreed with Natasha to give the Thames Ultra a go. This was a forty-five-mile stand-up paddleboard race from Henley to Teddington which allowed kayakers to take part. I was aware of it through yet another Yukoner, Joanne Hamilton-Vale, who was the race organiser. Nailing Natasha down to a race had previously proven difficult. Being

France-based, travelling over to race, let alone train, was tricky, and I think we were both acutely aware of how hard it can be to settle a boat with a different paddle partner. Nevertheless, we agreed a practice session in May on the River Trent to see how we fit, with the understanding that, if it worked out, we'd paddle the Thames Ultra together.

I got to the hotel near East Midlands airport at seven in the morning for that trial. Natasha had a plane to catch, and we needed to get a good ten miles in to be sure we would work. It was quite simply a magical morning. With all the people I have paddled marathon boats with over the years, it has taken months to reach a point of what rowers would call "swing", or the synchronicity where the paddling becomes so together, so effortless, that the boat almost feels like it is powering itself. When we pushed off from Beeston Lock and began paddling down the canal towards the Trent, we almost forgot we were paddling, we were just talking about all sorts of things, and not really concentrating on what the boat was doing. By the time we had completed the loop back up the river to Beeston Lock, I must have had the biggest, stupidest grin on my face. That "swing" was there. We had just got in and paddled, and it had just worked.

If I had a worry between then and the Thames Ultra, it was that I wasn't good enough to be a "co-equipier" in the boat. I was paddling with a multiple European and World champion in the driver's seat, and I felt like an impostor in the back. This was exacerbated by my relative lack of training, and that worry had grown considerably by the time we pitched up on the start line on June 15th in Henley. In all honesty, I don't think that fear was unjustified, and I was blowing fumes for a large portion of the race, but boy it was fun, and it was a really happy boat to be in. It was never quiet, from start to finish. We talked about anything and everything, and when we hit favourite films forty miles in, the paddler in the boat behind joined in too!

When we crossed the finish line, it felt like the most cathartic moment since finishing the Yukon River Quest. I was racing again, I'd survived an ultra, and best of all, I'd found a paddling soulmate in Natasha, if she was still prepared to paddle with me. That evening, as we sat in my parents' garden, I was in a state of bliss. All the work I'd been putting in to climb out of the hole that was the end of 2018 was finally beginning to bear fruit. That night, before retiring to my hammock, there was a moment that capped off the day, and finally set the shoulder issue to rest. Natasha took a look at my lats, found the knots in the muscles, and proceeded to work each and every one free. When I woke up the next morning, I felt in better shape than I had done prior to the race! What Leon had begun to correct with the industrial TENS machine, Natasha completed with her fingers. It immediately crossed my mind that she'd be the perfect third to paddle the R2AK, not least as she'd completed two channel crossings, one of which had been in pretty horrendous conditions. I think that in the end it was that crossing that decided for her that she wouldn't, but I'm sure, had she chosen to, we'd have made a formidable team.

Meanwhile, the planning process for 2020 was gathering pace. Along with Marieke, we booked on to a repeat of the smash and bash and navigation courses at Kingston in October, in part so Marieke could learn the same skills, and additionally for me to have a better chance of embedding the navigational skills. We also booked on to another advanced course with Roger for November. Over the summer I went back up to Anglesey for another course with Roger, aimed at surf and tide skills. I was getting more confident in my abilities to get back into a boat on my own, and while these sessions were group-based, my selfish goals were aimed at self-rescue. It was great to practice in the sea. My shoulder was no longer a major issue, and my fitness levels were on the up. We were to-ing and fro-ing with the R2AK team with questions about what was permitted in terms of sharing kit between solos. The responses were unsurprisingly sensible: emergency kit for each, sharing the less critical stuff was permitted.

It was a Friday in August that I had a message from Marieke asking for a Sunday pow-wow. This was nothing unusual. We were talking a lot about different aspects of the race, and it usually took a bit of an agenda and about half an hour a shot to talk things through. When I sat down that Sunday evening, I had no inkling of what was coming. Marieke started out. Work in the next six months was getting difficult, she said. There was a staff shortage, and she wasn't sure of the time off she could get. It was funny, but I started to get a whiff of what was coming. I'd never been dumped this way before, not for anything, and you could see the guilt on her face as it finally came out, and before the whammy hit, I knew it was coming. She'd been offered a seat in the Talisker Transatlantic race, she said, and it was with an all-Dutch crew with the aim of beating the women's record for the row. The strange thing was, I felt nothing at all, except possibly relief. Maybe I should have been angry, or upset, but it was almost a relief that she was bailing and leaving me enough time to regroup, and possibly find another partner, or at least reconcile myself to racing properly solo. I didn't even feel let down. In a strange way I found it amusing, just because I'd never been dropped like that before. It was a largely amicable parting of the ways for the race. She still came over for the courses we had booked and paddled with Roger in Anglesey. She never did make it to the Talisker, but we have kept in contact and remained friends.

Race entries for 2020 opened on 7th September 2019. Any race entry requires a team name, and mine had chosen itself off the back of that midnight sun experience at the Yukon. I'd long been a fan of the poet and artist, Giles Andreae. Back in the nineties, he'd published a series of irreverent poems and doodles on cards about things like "bottom burps" under the guise of "Purple Ronnie". In the noughties he'd morphed into Edward Monkton and produced a whole variety of stories and artwork, books, and films. I discovered him through his four-liner poems, with titles of the likes of "The Pig of Happiness", and "The Biscuit of Loveliness". The poem that really resonated with me was "Zen Dog":

He knows not where he's going,
For the ocean will decide -
It's not the DESTINATION...
...it's the glory of THE RIDE...

It was the last two lines that really struck a chord. It was almost a mission statement for the race entry: it doesn't matter what the outcome is; whatever happens the experience of taking part will be epic in its own right. Yukon was that kind of a life-affirming experience, and R2AK offered a chance to again capture a similar state of being.

However, I felt that I at least owed Giles the courtesy of asking permission to use the name, and when I emailed him, cheekily asked if it were possible to use the drawing and poem for the race. I honestly wasn't expecting a reply, let alone a prompt one. Within twenty-four hours he'd replied. "The privilege would be mine. What an endeavour!" He thanked me for asking and asked me to let him know what I needed. My team name was in the bag, and four days later my application to the vetting process had been submitted. This required a resume detailing what I'd done and what experience I had to merit getting a shot at the race. Despite my lack of sea experience, I reckoned I had a pretty good shot at getting through. The application form also asked for details of the boat. The answer to this was still open:

Now, here's the fun bit. I can't sort a boat until I know I'm in, as it's cheaper to buy there than ship, but when I'm in it'll almost certainly be a Seaward Quest X3 Kayak. As it's a kayak, when there's no wind, I'll move her faster!

By the 23rd, I'd passed the vetting stage and was able to complete the full enrolment process for the race. Things were beginning to get real. To enhance that reality, I contacted Steve Emery at Seaward Kayaks and by December had agreed a specification for the Seaward Quest X3 and placed an order. Although I knew they were based on Vancouver Island, not far from Victoria, I had no contingency for where to actually stash the boat once it was built. There were a number of very sketchy plans, some involving help I hadn't solicited from family in Vancouver, and another from friends over the border in the US, who I hadn't asked either. However, I needed a boat and couldn't rely on perfect lead times. I'd figure that out when the time required it. The same day I submitted the final order for the boat, in December, the official registration from the organisers came through.

Meanwhile, I had another sniff at being a prospective teammate, from a California-based Frenchman, Cyril Derreumaux, through Nicholas Goulden. We had an amiable conversation about the race, and our expectations of it. Cyril was a veteran of the race to Hawaii, a rowing race from California, and as part of a four-man crew he held the record for the fastest crossing, and as such I felt he was way out of my league. He helpfully provided information on nutrition, having run his own start-up selling adventure racing packs. Ultimately Cyril went off and chose to re-traverse the Pacific to Hawaii, only this time solo in a kayak. He became only the second person to achieve the feat after Ed Gillet in the eighties, making the crossing at his second attempt in the summer of 2022.

All the while this was going on, I was still working on my university course in the background. I knew that this was going to be in direct conflict for my attention to training and planning for my time in the States. Not only would I have to skip the summer semester for the race – there was no way I could complete papers around paddling the West Coast, but I was also going to have to skip the semester before to manage the trip logistics. This hit home in September and early October when I combined racing the Great Glen and Glasgow to Edinburgh Canoe Challenges with revision for what turned out to be the worst exam of my life – it was that bad I have never had the exam nightmare again. It was worth the trauma though. I paddled both events with Natasha, and while weather put an end to completing the Great Glen, which we paddled together in two sea kayaks, we combined in a two-man racing kayak to nail the Glasgow to Edinburgh. It was a fantastic weekend, with a less than auspicious start. We rocked up late, almost missing the start, and minus some compulsory kit – buoyancy aids – which we had to borrow from the local canoe club. However, on the water, and despite my navigational incompetence – how can you take a wrong turn when there's only one turn to make in the entire course? Entirely my fault – we beat allcomers. Winning, for me, was a first. Being a mixed crew and beating the men's crews was special; managing it in a happy boat was the icing on the cake. However, it came at the price of time for revision, so a hiatus was inevitable. University was parked after the exam, ostensibly for twelve months, as planning and training took over.

The courses Marieke and I had booked for November were still in play, and we went first to Kingston, and then up to Anglesey in November. It was an odd time, given Marieke was no longer on the R2AK team, but a fun couple of weekends, nonetheless. I left Howard Jeffs' courses in London more proficient at boat repair, and a smidgen above none the wiser for the navigation course. Anglesey was more productive. Working with Roger, I successfully managed several self-rescues in meatier swells than I'd been out in before. I was also getting increasingly comfortable paddling in gnarlier and gnarlier conditions.

In November, I ordered in NOAA charts for the West Coast from Canada. This was a big deal. Charts vary in scale and therefore detail, and there were an awful lot to choose from. What became very apparent when they arrived was that I wouldn't be able to take them with me. Not only did they consume masses of space, but they weighed a tonne too! Later, reading Susan Conrad's book on paddling the Inside Passage, she made it clear that she took a few maps at a time, and got the next set postal dropped en route. This was a non-starter as it contravened the race rules on outside support – you cannot have postal drops. However, it brought me as near as being over four thousand miles away from the race would allow, getting more of a feel for the route. Still, I'd only bought half the maps I'd need. I ended up getting the Garmin marine charts, which were to prove infinitely more useful before and during the race, but the maps of Juan de Fuca and the Broughton Islands make great wall hangings.

By Christmas, the tasks on the "urgent" pile were starting to grow. Over the Christmas break I spent many hours using the R2AK tracker to replay each and every human-powered team's route, and faithfully recreated those routes in Google Earth. By garnering all of these routes I was able to distil the results into one, most common route. Given my lack of knowledge of the West Coast waters, this gave me valuable insight into what path to take. The really fascinating bit wasn't that Mike of Team Mike's Kayak was so out there compared to all the other human-powered crews – he went up the outside, whereas everyone else went the more sheltered route – but that everyone else seemed to be *almost the same*, all the way.

2020 to 2021 : Delay

Everybody sit tight

All this time my training had been bubbling along in the background. I'd been putting in roughly thirty miles a week on the canal, with the odd race here and there to keep things spicy. By January this was not enough. As all good New Year's resolutions go, I kicked in with the heavy stuff on the first day of 2020. The regime was thus: six days a week, at six in the morning, I headed to the gym for thirty to forty-five minutes of rowing, running, or machine weights. In the evenings, there were ten miles to be completed on the canal, come rain or shine, and in almost all cases, come cold. In January, that meant getting on the water in the dark and adjusting to the ambient light. There was no sense in using a torch; the batteries would have cost a bomb, and in any case, the glare of the torch never carried as far as you needed and eclipsed everything you really needed to see. Besides, there's a perverse pleasure in paddling in the dark, as long as you avoid punting the local swans up their backsides. Even in those winter months the paddling itself was not a discomfort, as long as you had the right kit on. Neoprene pogie gloves were de rigueur, just to reflect the heat your hands gave off back on to themselves. The grim part was finishing. There was a minimal time gap between stopping padding, changing, and getting the boat back on the roof of the car where you remained warm. Inevitably by the time I was loading the boat, my hands would be numb, and had I been able to see them, almost certainly blue. It usually took a while in the bath to thaw out once home.

I was getting gym help from my friend, colleague, and partner in crime, Richard, who also came up with a genius idea for the boat. His suggestion was to start mimicking the gear I would carry in the boat by ballasting it with sandbags. He passed over a couple of hessian sacks into which we put around ten kilos of sand in plastic builder's bags. It meant no mess, and something that was soft and pliable enough to slide around in the hatches without damaging the boat. I added a couple of bags to the boat each session that February, totalling twenty-five kilos, and then in the following month doubled the weight. Given the Aquanaut has no rudder, this put an extra demand on my strokes to make sure the boat ran true. Well, when I say ran true, at least meandered in the right direction. When the second set of bags went in, this required extreme attention to the strokes. All of this compounded when coming anywhere near a moving narrowboat. Eighteen tonnes of narrowboat displaces a lot of water, and in a canal that really messes with the fluid dynamics of the water for hundreds of metres in front of the barge. When facing it in a kayak, the effect is to suck you towards the oncoming narrowboat, which is almost impossible to casually counter when paddling with no rudder to steer your craft. Weekend paddles when there was more water traffic were often the pits for this, but my night-time excursions were never affected, as narrowboats rarely move after dark. I also reasoned this was training hard to race easy, as I knew the Quest was equipped with a rudder, and salt water would make it more buoyant than the freshwater confines of the Ashby.

In late January my official race bio went live on the R2AK site. As with everything that is Race To Alaska, it was prosaic, eloquent, and a brilliant work of "faction":

At least until the day when The Handmaid's Tale gets re-classed as non-fiction, right now we live in an era when how you are born is less likely than ever to define how you get to be. For thousands of years most folks stayed ***one to none standard deviations*** *from how they plopped into the world. First born son of a king? From the screaming regal moment when they wipe the goop from your eyes and cut the cord, you're a king. Born into slavery? You're gonna spend your life enslaved. Unless you got the nod to sing the high hallelujah, whatever man and/or lady bits you got in the beginning dictated +/- what leading roles you were offered on the global stage. Haters gonna hate, and the struggle is still what it is and a million miles from fair and easy, but it's more possible than maybe ever to jump the line when biology and chance got it wrong and the thing you are is different than the born-to circumstances the world assigns.* ***Royals can chuck it all and move to Canada****; at least on this continent slavery is largely temporary and recreational;* ***surgeries, hormones, and RuPaul exist****. We're nowhere near judgment-free self-determination, but compared to the forever of human history, things seem to be loosening up.*

Our point? These days, ***even the English can become whitewater kayakers.***

Imagine the English countryside. What do you see? If you're like us, it's sheep, long rock fences, more sheep, and some ***old guy wearing tweed****. Imagine that's accurate, then imagine you are a young boy with* ***marmite-stained teeth*** *seeking the whitewater adrenaline of the Class 5 Colorado-style rapids depicted in the Mountain Dew commercials of the early 80s. You know you are meant for trick boating the canyons of the Rockies, to do the Dew, but you are trapped flatwater paddling in the* ***bucolic hellscape of Britain's rolling hills****. No hormones or surgery exist for that mismatch of self and circumstance.*

In an act of defiance and self-definition, Team Zen Dog didn't stuff down their truth, marry a beard, and learn to suffer in silence. Robert did what any ***courageous whitewater identifying person would do****: find the nearest elevation and water flow and start living into his truth.*

Since the 20-years-ago time when Team Zen Dog trained and then taught whitewater kayaking in the French Alps, this one-man voyage of self-actualization has unfolded himself to himself and the world, one paddle-stroked endurance race, one marathon, one hate and sufferfest event at a time. He's run up the Matterhorn and across entire countries (ok, Lichtenstein), paddled nonstop and 125 miles downriver (at least 8 times) on the Devizes to Westminster race, and the 444 miles of the Yukon River Quest. Why? Because ***that's Robert's true form****, and at least since 2014 he's been working up to the R2AK he saw when we nailed $10,000 to a tree.*

Despite his quest to find himself, we know he's found his tribe of fellow adventure-identifying hooligans because of his plan for his race vessel. From his application: "Here's the fun bit. I can't sort a boat until I know I'm in as it's cheaper to buy there than ship... but when I'm in it'll almost certainly be a Seaward Quest X3 Kayak."

He's going to buy his boat when he gets here for the race. ***That's R2AKAF****.*

A whitewater-identifying Englishman who has no idea what actual boat he's going to paddle, on the longest, most unsupported version of himself that he is aspiring to become? Regardless of how high your hackles got at the first paragraph of this thing, you've got to give a nod to the ***self-actualized spirit of adventure that*** *Team Zen Dog is living into, and that he might have landed the community who will welcome him as he is.*

Give us your tired, wet, and driven masses, longing to be free.

Welcome to the R2AK, Team Zen Dog. Like your same-named hotdog stand promises: we'll make you one with everything.

Courtesy of the Race to Alaska website

When this went live in the first week in February, I was contacted within a couple of hours by Ian Graeme from the legends that are team Oaracle about finding a boat. While it was too late an offer as the Quest was already built and sat in Seaward's yard, Ian did kindly agree to house it for me prior to the race. One of those seat-of-your-pants pieces of non-planning resolved itself in an instant. Moreover, Ian began providing some really comprehensive answers to questions I had on food, bailout plans, bears, navigation, providing me with links to all sorts of articles, and detailing his and Janice's own experiences and plans for previous races. Beyond Mike Higgins, this was the first real connection I had into the racer community, and it was a connection with an active racer at that.

Later that month I booked my flights to Canada. The skeleton plan was to go to Ian's, pick up the boat, and take it over to Port Townsend somehow, get my food dropped to friends in Sequim, and race. February, though, was beginning to unravel as the first cases of COVID were appearing in Britain. The Johns-Hopkins website started to show red blotches across the globe, not least including Washington State, and I was facing a very first-world problem about the race taking place. I began to re-open the communication channels with Dan Evans at Race Control; as if he had any better idea of what was coming than I did? The R2AK organisers continued to valiantly raise a middle finger to the quaking ball of phlegm COVID was spitting at them. "Race to Alaska is happening until it's not!". But I was getting increasingly uneasy.

By April the UK was in full lockdown. This meant that the canals and waterways were closed to boaters to protect the narrowboat residents who lived on them. My training was reduced to sessions on a Concept-2 rowing machine. Thankfully, as we were experiencing the most unseasonably warm and sunny of springs, I could do these out in the garden. But it was nowhere near the same as trolling up and down the waterways, and fitness-wise, I was losing ground on where I wanted to be.

That month, in myself I knew that the race would not happen that year. I made plans for its postponement by reactivating my university course. So cocksure was I, not only of race postponement, that I'd be furloughed, I signed up for not one but two course modules, a third of the whole thing in just six months. It took quite some self-discipline not to sign up for three. If I wasn't going to race, and I couldn't get on the canal, I'd fill my time productively. I wasn't to know then that I'd not be furloughed, and how intense the next twelve months were going to be.

On the last Friday that April the organisers pulled the race. With borders closing down there were some straight logistics in play which were at odds with 2020 happening. The key, I think, was the First Nations residents in Bella Bella. Westerners had brought them smallpox in the late 1800's and as a people with rightfully long memories, they weren't about to let a bunch of yahoos in boats bring another highly contagious and potentially fatal virus with them a hundred and fifty years on. The inevitability of the decision to cancel didn't detract from how gut wrenching it was. Still, first-world problems and all that... This was a postponement, not a cancellation.

There were some basic decisions to be made. I'd quit alcohol to race and had been dry for nearly a year and a half. Should I start drinking again? I rationalised that being locked down and drinking again would be a bad combination, so I decided to lay off for another twelve months. It wasn't a hard decision to make.

That summer was hard, but I know I was comparatively lucky compared to others who were furloughed or lost their jobs. I kept working throughout the pandemic. Losing access to the canal to train did set in motion a chain of events that nearly undid me. As training was curtailed, and half hours on the rowing machine weren't cutting it, I lost my sleep patterns. I'd crash at ten, only to wake at one and not be able to zonk out again. Combined with losing that year's race, not being able to paddle with old paddle partners, stress from work projects not going to plan, and what was for me the claustrophobia of being cooped up in close proximity to others – I know, I shouldn't have felt that way about my family, but I did – took me to a seriously dark place that August. I was coping with race withdrawal by watching the clips of the day for human powered crews from previous years over and over again. I think I must be responsible for more than half the hits on the videos for Solveig, Backwards AF and Heart of Gold, not to mention the tracker junkie clips.

When the canals finally reopened that summer, I got myself back out at the first possible opportunity. It was surreal to be back on the water, and for my first two sessions I saw nobody, not a narrowboat resident nor any walkers on the towpaths. On my third paddle I finally encountered two friends who lived on the Black Pearl narrowboat at Sutton Cheney Wharf. "Where have you been?", they asked. I explained I'd been following the Waterways and Canoe England's lockdown guidance, and not been on the canal. It transpired I'd been in a minority! They'd seen every man and his kayak out on the water. Loads of people had ignorantly just gone out and paddled.

As a result of August's mental dip, I sought out paddlers to help keep me right. Jen Clough was an acquaintance dating back to racing on the Dordogne in France. Actually, to be fair, we were more acquaintances from a very messily alcoholic celebration of the entente cordiale and Liberation Day from the day after the race. We started bi-weekly paddles in Oxford.

This also meant having someone to sound off for sea kayaking advice, and really steadied me at a time it was desperately needed.

By the time I'd got to October, I'd nailed all the papers the university course required, and took the gamble to complete it by April, reasoning I could handle the project alongside training if push came to shove. In retrospect, had R2AK 2021 gone ahead, this would have compromised the race and the course. In the event, it meant that by April 2021 I had one less plate to spin. The organisers pulled R2AK 2021 in December 2020. There was no last-minute decision this time. I was able to mothball full training and race planning for the winter. I carried on getting out on the water, but with nothing like the intensity ultra-paddling demanded.

2021 was a funny old year. I raced with Jen in the Norfolk Ultra, which we won. It would be lovely to say we deserved to win it, but the race was the same day as the National's and virtually nobody showed up. Still, you have to be in it to win it. We went and raced the Great Glen together, in plate-glass conditions, which was just as well as we gambled with a fairly stable racing kayak rather than a sea boat. Glasgow to Edinburgh was back, and it seemed churlish not to go and race that as well, solo this time. Although COVID had us dipping in and out of lockdown, I was finding targets and ticking off races, and it felt good. I am really grateful to Jen for putting up with me; the races were fun, and I had my paddling mojo back. By the time I completed the Ross Warland Memorial that December I was back in the right frame of mind for Alaska.

Getting time away from work was another consideration. I applied for two months' unpaid leave, and after no small number of consultations was granted it. I was that committed to the project that I think, had work said "No", I would have quit to race. I'm grateful that it never came to that.

By October, a fringe benefit of the enforced race delay was turning into a major asset. My cousin Helen had relocated to Denver with her husband, Steve, and were offering race help. You know there's something special about your cousin when she sends you birthday presents addressed to "My cousin who is a knob", and Helen is extra-special because she is super, super organised, especially in comparison to my project management activities. Helen was stepping in with offers of help on, among other things, logistics and food acquisition, and was starting to question – and validate – some of my decisions for the race. Having someone focus you really helps, and both Helen and Steve were going to be pivotal in this role over the next few months.

I still managed the odd trip over to Anglesey to paddle. In all the sessions up until November, I'd paddled under instruction, or I'd paddled in a group. That month, I went out and did my first solo paddles. These were long overdue, and an immediate "whoa!" When you paddle solo, it's apparent that the safety net of others, illusory or otherwise, is not there. I'd done all the self-rescue practice under Roger's watchful eye, but this was very different. There is a definite mindset required to paddle solo. For my first outing alone, I chose to paddle from Rhoscolyn Bay to Trearddur Bay and back. To begin with, my butt cheeks were shaking as I nervously picked out points on the coast, and just paddled to them, but by the end of the session I was sitting comfortably and paddling further from shore.

I was still devouring as much information as I could get on the Inside Passage. Denis Dwyer's books had been a good start point, and Susan

Conrad's book "Inside" was absorbing. I found out about the kayaker's lodge, the "Magical Cabin" at Burnett Bay, below Cape Caution. YouTube yielded a plethora of home videos of coastal trips, Danny Ami's and Dam Good Trips being among the best, and at least one good series detailing history of various points along the way. It also turned up a recording of Ian and Janice's webinar, complete with full trip risk assessment. Being four thousand miles away meant that this was the best I could get at a distance, and I was grabbing hold of anything and everything I thought might help.

2022 : Countdown

Prepare for events that are coming…

As 2022 began I re-instigated the R2AK training plan. Richard again helped me by setting out a gym routine for the mornings, HIIT sessions and circuits, while the evenings were set for canal sessions, and I had a similar set provided by Max Kimberley. It was a wrench, stepping into the ultra-training regime, as getting up before six in the morning in the dark was just plain hard. Similarly, after work, it required a strength of will just to drive to the canal and get on the water in the dark. Once on the water it was simple. The sessions were all ten miles, either heading one way through town, or the other out to the aqueduct. Richard helped, as did Jim, another gym regular, just by being there to train with in the mornings.

The rationale in the session structure is simple: in having no more than twelve hours between sessions for six days a week, your body adapts to the relentlessness of the training, and you get used to minimal recovery times, and your stamina builds. Two weeks into the year, I was sleeping as deeply as I could want, consciousness clicking off like a light switch when my head hit the pillow in the evening, and sharply back on when my alarm summonsed me to the gym in the morning. The body, however, doesn't take kindly to this at the outset. I was having to revisit the gym plans, as my lateral and trapezoid muscles in my shoulders and back were knotting up, painfully so. I replaced calisthenics and weights in the gym with runs and bike sessions, and enlisted the help of Twig, an elite triathlete and physio, who once a week gave my back a sports massage to get rid of the knots and keep them at bay. The routine was settled: sixty miles a week in the boat, and by mid-February, even with an additional twenty-five kilos of sand in the boat, I was beginning to feel fitter. It was always a good feeling finishing a session on Thursday evening, knowing Friday was rest day, being able to enjoy recovery and a lie-in, and just as good hitting the end of Sunday's session, knowing the week was complete. When I threw in positives of the sports massages on Tuesday nights, there was something else to look forward to nearly every other day. I was enjoying training, always a healthy sign that things are going right.

Training has its upsides. Ashby Canal at dawn. Most of my training was on the confines of the canal, ten metres wide and one deep. A far cry from the sea.

The worry of COVID was ever-present. I'd had the deferral of my race entry from 2020, and Air Canada had generously, I felt, refunded my flights from that year. I'd resubmitted that entry in the autumns of both 2020 and 2021, but you always felt the threat of another lockdown, or of catching COVID, or worse, long COVID, and having your training plans scuppered. It was quite a moment when my race bio was republished in mid-February, almost verbatim from 2020. Booking flights to Vancouver in February felt both like a leap of faith in the race, and a vote of confidence by me that it would actually happen. I had to decide how long I was going to be gone for, too. I decided to give myself the best part of a fortnight before the race, primarily to prepare and get used to the boat. It also meant I could plan for how to get it from where it was in Victoria down to the start line. Flights were booked. Shit was getting very real.

Planning didn't stop. There was food to consider. I'd got a dehydrator and vacuum bagger in the UK without properly thinking through that shipping home-made food to North America was a bad idea on so many levels. I got the same kit and shipped it to Helen in Denver, with the intention of going down the home-made line with her help. We started talking recipes, but never got that far. By March she was nagging me for recipes to cook. Helen steered me towards pre-packed meals on Amazon, in the end probably the best call. Mountain House and Peak were hitting the calorie levels I wanted, and I found plenty of calories in Clif bars, which looked very suitable, not least because they appeared in photos from Backwards AF's blog on their voyage in 2019. Greenbelly breakfast bars looked promising for the mornings. I cannot stomach porridge, and these were an oaty, not entirely dry alternative. I added Snickers bars, because you need the psychological boost of having chocolate bars in your locker. I then started a spreadsheet detailing meals and snacks, their weights in grammes, and their calorie values. These I broke into meals and snacks to try and get enough stacked in for a daily intake. By mid-March there was a substantial food order on its way to Denver. Helen supplemented this with a visit to Costco, where she picked up enough nuts, raisins and assortments to sink the boat with trail mix. Food was on track.

Then there was the route. I knew the lines I was going to follow, and some alternatives depending on the weather, but I was not entirely up to speed with where to camp. I revisited all the human-powered endeavours from previous years and marked in Google Earth where they'd pitched up every night. I then hit the BC Marine Trails website, which was detailed both in Susan Conrad's and Denis Dwyer's books and started pinning these into Google Earth too. I'd been getting a lot of questions from friends and colleagues by this stage about bears and camping, and was mindful of this in locating sites. Helpfully, at around this time, Denis Dwyer posted some advice in the Inside Passage Sea Kayakers forum on Facebook on this subject. Camp on small islands where there's no fresh water source, like streams, they said, because in summer bears will be congregating on streams to fish and not bothering with those little islands. This sounded really good to a newbie like me until someone pointed out that mummy bears sometimes take their cubs out to those islands to protect them from boar. Boar? I already had bears, wolves, sealions and orca to contend with. Now the list had gotten longer.

I was watching the R2AK site to see who I was contending with. This would have a bearing on who I could expect to have in the vicinity for the race. As the entry deadline drew nearer, it became apparent that there were going to be very few solo human-powered crews taking part. For a short while I believed it would only be me. Then, at the last minute, Team Interstice appeared on the roster, a solo rowing boat sculled by a Washingtonian - Lilian. I can't recall if that felt like a relief, or whether I was put out at not being the only solo human powered entrant (which would have been daft, but that's probably just me). When the entries closed, there were two two-man row boats, one two-man kayak, the rower, and me. Hindsight and previous race rosters dictated that this was to be expected, but I had thought there'd be more. At least for the first leg, an event in its own right, there was one other kayaker in Team Arm and Leg.

I can vividly recall my mother's reaction when she found out I was the only solo kayak. I'd already made the mistake of showing her the Race to Alaska movie, which if you want to feel reassured about your son's safety was always going to have the opposite effect. Finding out that I was unlikely to be anywhere near other boats: Well. Another mistake. My bad. Sorry mum.

For April I booked a bespoke mid-week course with Roger Chandler back in Anglesey. This was a one-to-one session with Roger, nobody else in the group. By the week it took place, conditions were looking unsettled. Roger gave me the choice of a calmer day on the Friday rather than the Thursday, or work in the Swellies. The Swellies are essentially the Menai Straits, a tidal channel that flows in opposite directions every six hours. I opted to stick with the Swellies plan. While the Menai Straits aren't on a par with what Seymour Narrows can offer, they are a challenge in their own right, and unbelievably I'd never got to paddle them before.

Menai Straits under Pont Britannia. Courtesy of Roger Chandler

I went to meet Roger under the Menai Suspension Bridge that Thursday morning, and we shuttled our kayaks down to the Sea Zoo at the West End of the Straits. I chose to paddle with sand ballast to replicate the weight of gear in the boat, and we headed East down to the bridges. It was a confidence-certifying day. We worked the currents from one side of the Straits to the other, and then made our way down the centre of the channel past the fish trap to the old bridge. From there Roger started setting me challenges, to get back upstream to Britannia Bridge by working the eddies, surfing the small race that appeared at Ynys Benlas, and playing on the currents under the old bridge. It was challenging, but I was rising to it all and I felt, if not in control, comfortable in where my abilities lay relative to the water I was on. I backed this up the following day with a solo paddle across Cymyran bay from Rhosneigr to Rhoscolyn and back. It was still a challenge to reconcile myself to being alone on the water, but as a final sea preparation went prior to heading out to North America, it was a tonic I required.

Ten days later was a different yet familiar challenge, this time with a twist. Easter weekend brought the Devizes to Westminster Canoe Race. Through injury and weather, this was my first participation on the water for five years. It always feels arrogant to say it, but for me this was a training run, not a race, and to spice it up I decided to forego the racing boat for the Aquanaut. Paddling a sea kayak on the Kennet and Avon Canal and the Thames brings a different set of challenges. Principally, the Aquanaut weighs in nearly four times heavier than the racing shell. This would require a lot of grunt, and add a lot of time with seventy six portages around locks to complete. I got a set of wheels, and some Velcro straps to set them up on the back as a permanent fixture for the race. I did have car roof straps as a backup. I'll unhappily admit I'd not tried out this get-up prior to taking part, but this was only training, right?

At the first portage I heaved the boat out of the water and flipped it onto the wheels. As I tentatively began pulling it up the side of the lock towards the gate it felt solid, and I relaxed, began to accelerate. Right up until the wheels hit a ridge in the path and all four Velcro straps simultaneously and audibly disintegrated, leaving the boat blocking the way. All of this was right in front of another crew, and of all crews to block, the visually impaired one. Another inauspicious start for Team McCall.

Velcro wasn't going to cut it. The roof straps went on and, with a further ten minutes lost a while later optimising the wheel set-up, the mounting issue was sorted. I began a portage routine: pull in at the lock and get out. Lift the boat from the front and pivot it up on to the bank. Flip over on to the wheels. Grab the front toggle and walk purposefully to the get in. Then reverse the flip/pivot process and get in. This worked fine except where the banks were steep, and I had at least one inelegant tumble and slide to the water's edge, but thankfully no swim.

Devizes to Westminster: Dawn at Longridge on Day Two. Courtesy of Alison Hardy

A few locks later, as I came to land, I was horrified to see that one of the wheels had lost its retainer and was precariously wobbling on the end of its axle. This looked like one problem I couldn't fix with gaffer tape. As my pit crew were several locks away, I modified the get out/put in routine to include the retrieval, mounting, dismounting, and stashing of the wheel using the front hatch. Having Mike on pit crew was invaluable. After that day, we had a proper engineering solution for the rest of the event. I was never going to trouble the leader board in the Aquanaut, and it turned into a congenial weekend with friends on and off the water. It was great after COVID to be able to paddle with others in a racing environment again, and bore the socks off old acquaintances talking about paddling.

Devizes to Westminster was instrumental to my training plans in that, for three days that spring, it increased my daily workout from ten to closer to thirty five miles. I went in with no real taper from the weekly plans, save dropping one day's gym and paddle two days before it began. If Race to Alaska was the mountain I was going to climb, these days were the foothills that tested out that I was in reasonable shape, and I was. However, having navigated my way to and through the foothills, and being all of eight weeks from the start, I was now stood at the bottom of the mountain. From five years out it looked epic and inviting, but distant. Now, here I was, within touching distance of the start, standing at the bottom and gazing upwards. It looked... overwhelming.

I had to adjust training to allow time to knock off the jobs that needed to be done, and there was a pile of them. Plot additional campsites, plot water sources, pack kit, ship kit, sort clothes... There was plenty to do, and faffing time was very limited and definitely finite. I had collected all my gear in two large plastic war chests in my office. Last-minute items were Amazon-ing their way in there: ginger tablets, waste dry sack, AA lithium batteries, dry boxes... I spent hours back on US and Canadian websites finding more possible camping places. Google Earth felt like it should be helpful but was only good for doing so when saving location files.

I was talking with Ian Graeme more by now. He was sending me updates from Victoria, where the weather was decidedly unusual. The photographs of the sea states off Victoria he sent were not reassuring.

Preparations still included practice, and that covered camping. I slung the hammock between the kids' old play fort and an ash tree in the border in the garden and spent the first week of May sleeping out there. All was going well until a week in, when I was woken by a loud crash at one in the morning. I lay there for a couple of minutes trying to figure out what had happened. It sounded like a fairly major car crash as it seemed to have come from the direction of the road. I rolled over – to discover that I was no longer suspended in the hammock but lying on the ground. Oh. At least now I knew where the noise had come from. I extricated myself from the folds of the hammock and the tarpaulin which had covered it to find that the feet of the tower the hammock was attached to had given way. The legs had reached a critical rotted state just above the metal anchors and the whole tower unit, given the pull from the hammock cords, had toppled over towards me, and while gently lowering me to the ground, missed my head my inches. It took a sizeable effort to shift the tower from the canvas. I would never have known what hit me and joined the Darwin Award list had it done so. I debated retiring to the house but decided that explaining what had just transpired was best left to the following day. Besides, there was an opportunity to try the hammock in its alternative mode as a bivi. I adjusted the lines and hoops, crawled back inside, and went back to sleep.

There was one part of the pack list I'd not really given too much thought to, not in terms of quality but quantity, and that was clothes. Over three years I'd accumulated thermals, Vaikobi tops and leggings, Sealskinz socks, hats and gloves. I had enough to mount a major expedition to the South Pole, but the volume it would take up? I revisited Denis Dwyer and Susan Conrad's books, seeking out what was a sensible amount of clothing to take, knowing deep down the answer. Cue two and a half boat changes, and enough clothes for three days off the water. Launderettes would feature regularly on the trip, and life was going to be smelly, if not for me, then certainly for those around me. All of this condensed into one twenty-litre dry bag and what was on me.

With two weeks to go before my flights I took two actions. Firstly, I went into self-quarantine and started working from home. There was no way I wanted to get taken out by COVID at this late stage. Secondly, I shipped the camping gear ahead. The hammock, tarpaulins, sleeping bag, the cooking kit and sundry camping items all went in a duffel bag, and went on ahead to Ian's place. It was a gamble, but I figured two weeks was plenty of time for it to clear Canadian customs.

I then spent several days planning a practice paddle from Victoria over to Port Townsend, allowing for three different routes through the San Juan Islands, marking all the campsites I could find. On my penultimate weekend at home, I loaded all three Garmin units with the routes and waypoints. The electronic mapping was complete. This left two jobs: physical maps and getting competent with my VHF radio.

VHF is an R2AK prerequisite. They don't say exactly what you need, other than a VHF radio is required, but it seemed logical that being able to use it was part of that requirement. I'd signed up for the Royal Yachting Association VHF course in 2019 but had never got round to completing it. Common sense, hindsight and plenty of other sensible things dictate I should have done these sessions ages ago but, more fool me, I hadn't. It was online, and at dawn on the last Monday, I raced through it. Immediately I had some problems. The radio I'd brought in 2019 wasn't registered with Ofcom, which was a legal requirement. I was on the Ofcom registration site, so this was done, certificate printed and with the radio duly legalised, within a few minutes I was printing out the course completion document. It transpired from "next steps" in the course that course completion was the final step to... the exam. Bugger. This was eight days before going. Where was I going to sit an exam? I had visions of spending at least one day in my last weekend driving to Southampton or Portsmouth to sit one, which was time I didn't want to lose.

In desperation I dropped Paul Lewis a message. Paul is a work colleague, and he'd steered me to the VHF unit I'd bought for the trip. Paul was back very promptly. No problem. In yet another lucky break, it transpired that Paul was a certified Royal Yachting Association examiner for VHF. Later that week he put me through my paces, and I passed. I had the theory and the bare minimum of practice in the bag. I packed the radio manual so I could learn how to use the unit I had in the time I had in Canada and the US before the race.

This left the maps. In the final weeks, I'd gotten hold of the tide information for as many waypoints as possible on my route. I'd taken screen grabs of my maps, complete with campsite information, superimposed routes, freshwater points, and overlaid the tidal charts. This was a simple job for the outset of the race. I knew what day I'd be taking on Juan de Fuca, Oak Bay... but by the time I was supposed to be at the North end of Vancouver Island, this was fanning out to cover days, if not weeks. By the time I was done I had eighty pages of maps. Late on the last Friday, I went into the office, taking with me sixty sheets of tearproof, waterproof A3 paper, and printed my copy using laser printers. This was Mike Higgins at his most influential. As he reasoned, laser printing is done by fusing toner powder to paper with a heat-lamp, and it is naturally waterproof. Put this on waterproof, tearproof paper and bingo! I took a couple of trial maps and ran them under the taps and gave it my best shot to rip them. They took up far less space and weighed a fraction of the NOAA charts I had at home. They fit the bill, and the map case, just. The only issue was that they held so much static, it was difficult to remove them from the map case, and then sort them. Yet I had my backup: proper nautical charts with a compass, and the routes and bearings.

I love my work colleagues.

It was a calculated risk, breaking quarantine that day. I did step into the office to say goodbye to the few colleagues that were there, and there was one final surprise. On my desk was a box of cakes with the message "please don't die" - with a smiley face - on top. The race had been drumming up interest over the preceding months and I'd had plenty of questions, mostly about what I was going to do to avoid being eaten by bears. This was a touching surprise from Kate, on whom I was dumping most of my responsibilities and coding skeletons for the next two months. It was as good a sign-off from work as I could have wanted. I took a picture of the cakes and posted it in my team group on Facebook with the caption "I love my work colleagues", which is true. I picked up my VHF exam pass from Paul, and I was done with work. Shit had just got very, very real.

That weekend I packed the remaining bags, another duffle bag, and a paddle bag that consumed both sets of paddles and then, tardis-like, all sorts of sundry items. All the electronica went in hand luggage. It felt strange to be flying with so much electronic safety gear: EPIRB, VHF radio, Garmins, chargers in hand luggage, and I was genuinely concerned that it might get confiscated at airport security. I was done. Training and preparation were complete. I was now right at the foot of the mountain. Time to go. I went to Heathrow a day early so there were no dramas with the flight. I was aware by now that the bag I'd shipped ahead was stuck in Calgary, in customs, awaiting clearance. The two weeks I'd bargained were sufficient for its arrival had gone. I was concerned yet it was not yet a huge headache. I still had a week to play with.

2022 : Green Light

Ignition sequence starts

I arrived in Vancouver with thirteen days to go until the race. I spent my first night with Cousin Jim and Vicky in Richmond, and the following morning Jim dispatched me on the bus to Victoria and to Ian Graeme. Conversations with Ian had been sporadic over the last two years, but if there was ever a gauge as to what he was like, it was what he'd done for me with my boat. I caught a taxi to Ian's from the bus station. His house was easy to spot. The Oaracle two-man rowing boat was parked on the drive, and there were bits of boat everywhere. Ian welcomed me in for what was to be four nights staying with him. My immediate impression was one of just about organised chaos. Ian seemed to be doing everything for everybody else, including me, and then last-minute fitting in the jobs he needed to get done so he and Janice could race. This began with fixing up the rowboat, which Carling was racing with Michelle as Team Let's Row Maybe? (after the Carly Rae Jepsen song, apparently) and whom Ian had helped get together not long before from the remains of two other potential teams. I met Carling that afternoon too, as she came over to work on the boat. You could feel that Olympian aura – the drive – emanating from her. She was quiet - we barely said a word to each other. I guess that she was probably shy. I was definitely in awe.

First up was meeting my boat, Minnie. Minnie was named after my grandmother's nickname for me. When I'd been the smallest in my house my uncle had called me "Minimus", and my grandmother had persisted in calling me "Min", even when I was six feet four and she was no longer troubling five feet. As the smallest in the fleet, it seemed an apt choice for the Quest. Ian had her down in the garage along with assorted other craft, still in pristine condition. He'd joked over the winter that it had been lost in the floods, and I'd retorted that it was probably just under the big pile of dust in the corner.

I spent the first day prepping her up, adding the decals my niece Katie had produced for me with Edward Monkton's poem. I ran the poem once down each side of the boat, with the Zen Dog picture on the front hatch, and just behind the stern one. Katie had also produced me my four horses. This is a long-standing Devizes to Westminster joke about what it takes to complete endurance races: the strength of a racehorse, the stamina of a carthorse, the brains of a rocking horse, and the stubbornness of a donkey. These went around the front hatch. I added several GoPro mounts, not for cameras, but for the Garmin units and the SPOT trackers. The standard seat came out, and in went the memory foam seat in its square dry bag. I packed the dry sacks I'd brought with the gear and started to fill Minnie up. This was Krypton factor territory. I was running trips up from and down to the garage, still paring down kit I'd brought with me. There were still two major kit issues. My camping equipment had not arrived through the courier I'd used to transport it over, and I had a list of gear I needed to acquire in Victoria. Items like gas, matches, bear spray and flares do not sit well with flying and security, so a trip to the Mountain Equipment Centre was in the offing. Still, packing the boat that day was the beginnings of what was to be a strained relationship between me and my kit.

I was here! I'd arrived and was locked into the race now, and more importantly I'd met the first of the race legends in Ian. He's impossible not to like. It goes without saying he has that Canadian "nice" gene, and he was easy to get on with. Conversations ranged from the race to Jonathan Pie, rowing, politics, all sorts. I showed him my maps which I think he found amusing. He showed me the Oaracle equivalent, and I felt for a minute that maybe I'd gone overboard in my map preparation. The Oaracle maps came on the form of a long, I think taped together, toilet roll-wide strip that went on and on for about four metres. They were considerably less detailed than mine, but common sense would tell you that Oaracle had considerably more local and prior race knowledge of the course. Every now and then through the week, Ian would share an anecdote from previous races, such as being followed by a cloud of insects from one camp location near Bella Bella. These were all nuggets I was trying to absorb. Anything that made this possible was going to help, and I had no idea if I'd see Ian and Janice much during the race.

I spent the next two days to-ing and fro-ing to Victoria to get the kit. There was the missing camping and safety kit, and basics like painkillers and sunblock for the boat. I'd decided to skip the bear canisters in favour of hoisting my food, after discussion with Ian, although Lilian had kindly offered me a spare canister before I'd arrived. There were other sundries like a sim for my phone, the absence of which was causing me no end of grief. I got to see where Stage One finished, and Stage Two started, down by the Empress Hotel in Victoria Harbour. It still felt unreal, but I was now here.

On the Friday we went for a swim and a row, and I finally got to properly meet Janice. The odd couple, Ian and Janice? Maybe. Another Olympian, Janice was another reserved but genuinely lovely person. Where Ian appeared maybe less organised, Janice was someone who struck me as well-regimented and super-planned, and very tidy. I hope I'm not doing Ian too much of a disservice in saying she's the rock of the team, but then he does refer to her as the JMPU, the Janice Mason Power Unit. Having a lesson on a Lite-Boat rowing boat from them was a blast, and I hope one that Uncle Pete, who had been the rower in our family, was looking down on. I didn't swim, and it was actually quite fun powering a boat in a direction where I could barely see where I was going. I'd consider more rowing on the back of that experience.

By Saturday I had all of my gear, save the main pile of food and some small boat repair bits. It had reached the point I needed to be on the move again. My original plan had been to paddle across Haro Strait just to the East of Victoria, through the San Juan Islands, and down the West Coast of Whidbey Island to Port Townsend. Recognising that I was crossing the US border and the necessity to check in with US Customs, I'd been planning on using one of the online apps, CBP Roam or CBP One, to make my registration. However, I'd not fully investigated what I needed to do with either app, or what either app was capable of letting me register.

That morning, I opened the CBP One app. It immediately became clear that it was incomplete; the "Sea" option linked to a "Coming Soon" message. While there was the possibility of fudging it by using another menu, my alarm bells were ringing, and Ian rightly pointed out that it was probably sensible to talk to US Customs in Roche Harbor - the first point I'd land at on San Juan Island - to at least give them a heads up on my intended route.

I phoned Roche. Miraculously for a Saturday afternoon, they answered. I explained to the customs officer on the other end what my intended route and entry into the US was. He was friendly and responded by asking me what paperwork I had for the crossing. Passport, ESTA, surely that was all that was required? Apparently not: I also needed an I94, which Roche

Harbor couldn't issue me with. It turns out that the I94 is the stamp you get in your passport once you have been photographed and fingerprinted by US Border Control.

The customs officer directed me to speak to US Preclearance in Victoria. Given I needed the paperwork as soon as possible, I jumped on a bus and headed over to the pre customs office in James Bay, and not without some trepidation. Everything I'd heard about US Border Customs came with a complete lack of humour.

I knocked on the customs office door to be greeted by an unsmiling armed officer. I explained to him the conversation I'd had with Roche Harbor and asked if I could get the I94 sorted with them. This must have been an extremely unusual request, because he called a couple of his colleagues over for their opinions, and I explained again. No, this was not possible. They couldn't just give me an I94 to paddle over the border when I felt like it. They had to know I'd made the crossing and was in the US. Not even a stop at Roche to register was enough. The only way for me to get the I94 was to go through a registered port where they could process me. As conversations with officialdom went, it was pretty intimidating even asking about possibilities, and it was clear to me that there was no point in arguing the toss. Sunday's plan was scuppered. I would have to change them.

Back at Ian's we looked at the options. The ferry to Anacortes, which would have got me at least on to part of my route, was closed through either lack of staff, lack of demand, or that usual blame hound - COVID. There were no ferries from Tsawwassen to the US, and the only feasible route was the Black Ball ferry from Victoria over to Port Angeles. The San Juan route was sadly off the agenda. I needed to come up with a new plan based on the

North Olympic coast to get used to paddling my kayak, and all the shore-based tasks I was going to have to complete at the beginning and end of each day.

We ferreted out the campsites between Port Angeles, where the ferry docked, and Port Townsend. I don't know why I expected to find more, but they were scarce on the shoreline. There was one at the foot of Dungeness Spit, which looked attractive as it was located right on the shoreline. Further round, at probably a 30-mile paddle, was the Sequim Bay State Park campground, which seemed to be inland and probably difficult to get to because of hills. Port Townsend had Fort Worden, and as campsites went it appeared it would have plenty of space.

The other issue I now had was moving the boat on land. As my plan had been to beach camp en route, dragging the boat out and in negated any need for wheels. Now I had to contend with the ferry with a fully laden kayak weighing in at close to a hundred kilos. Ian kindly dug out a set I could borrow for the trip to Port Townsend. As Heath Robinson plans went, this was flimsy, but I had a straight route along the coast, some stopping points, enough food for a week, and a solution to the I94 problem. It was time to get paddling again.

2022 : Stateside – 12 Miles

Eight...Seven...

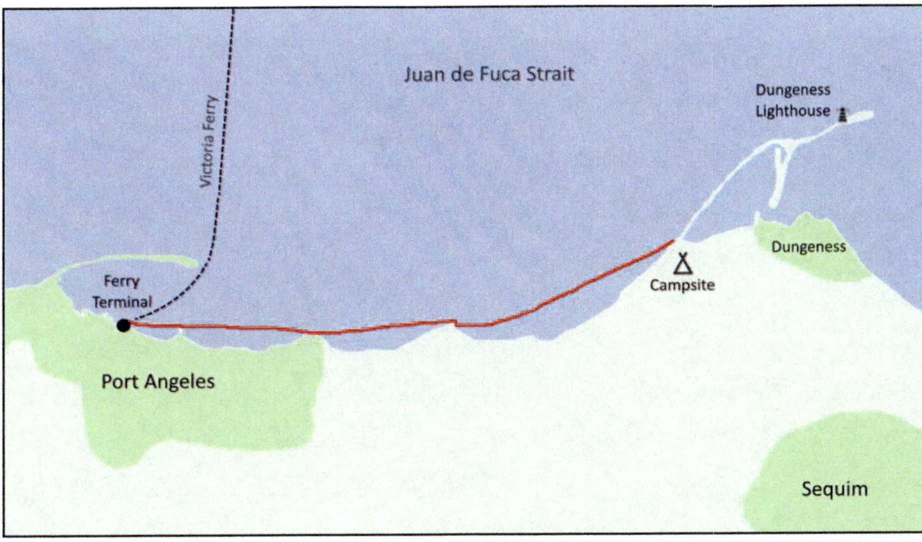

Ian drove me down to the ferry terminal early Sunday morning. I loaded up the dry sacks into the hatches while Ian sorted out mounting Minnie on the wheels. We discovered that one of the tyres had a flat, so Ian went off in search of an open garage to pump it up, but to no avail. Given the boat had to make it on and off the ferry we figured that it would do the job. Little did I know that would come back to haunt me later that day. Having checked with the ferry staff where kayaks should go, we wheeled the boat into the departure terminal. It felt as embarrassingly conspicuous as riding a bike through a building to be dragging a boat into the passenger terminal. I got my ticket, said my goodbyes and thanks to Ian, and sat down, wondering which door and ramp Minnie was going to manage to get through to get on the boat. So, apparently, did the shore staff, who then redirected me back out the terminal entrance, and down to the motorbike area. The US pre customs officer from the previous day reappeared with a surprisingly friendly handshake, went through the process of photographs and fingerprints (no board with numbers on it though… I felt just short of being criminalised), and with the flat wheel rolled lopsidedly onto the ferry.

By the Blackball Ferry, Victoria. The wheels were more problematic on than off.

The crossing from Victoria to Port Angeles is about twenty miles. As we got further away from Vancouver Island, I tried to get a snapshot in my head of the peaks around the city, so that I'd have a clue what I was aiming for eight days hence. I then got my first sighting of the Olympic Peninsular up ahead. There were bluffs where I was headed, extending as far as I could see off to the East. I began to wonder if this was going to be an issue for landing later in the day.

When I landed in Port Angeles I trundled up the ramp, and straight into the finish of the Olympic Marathon, which as luck would have it was in full swing and had its post-race area set up across the front of Hollywood Beach, right where I'd set my put-in point. I successfully navigated through the various barriers and runners and on to a small slip, filled up my dromedaries (water bladders) in the Feiro Marine Centre, and rather self-consciously began to kit up. Drysuit, wet boots, deck and buoyancy aid went on, and maps, GPS and food went on deck, all in front of plenty of probably disinterested marathoners and spectators. I then rolled Minnie down to the water, tied the wheels on top of the rear hatch, and slid her out. It wasn't lost on me that this was the first time I'd ever paddled her, and that the trip was a solo one on a stretch of sea I'd never set eyes on before. I switched on my VHF and the Garmin unit, and pushed out, heading beyond the old loading jetty that blocked my direct path along the coast. It was raining, and there was a Westerly wind to supplement the incoming tide that I was riding toward Dungeness Spit, so other than the roll of the waves, the conditions were in my favour.

After an hour I headed into the beach beyond East Port Angeles, in the lee of the wind and sheltered from the waves. Minnie was paddling beautifully, but the water bottle on my buoyancy aid was already empty and I was full. I emptied and refilled, had a couple of snacks and headed off again. It was tonking rain by now and the wind was picking up. By the time I got to the bottom of Dungeness Spit the waves were running at nearly three feet, and I was beginning to feel seasick. I realised as I came in that I'd need to be out of the boat as quickly as possible on landing and went to pop my deck off, only to find I'd made the elementary error of sealing the toggle loop used to release the deck inside the boat. Not a clever move, and another reminder of how green a sea kayaker I was. Thankfully I'd left enough time to remedy that, and the cockpit cover was off as I hit the shingle.

The boat swung sideways and over, and I scrambled out. The cockpit filled with water, which only added to the effort of dragging an already heavy tank clear of the waves. Inelegant crash landing this definitely was. It took me several minutes to get the boat clear of the breaking waves, and a few more to get her on the wheels again.

As I looked up, I realised I now had another problem. The campsite was clearly not rolling down on to the beach: it was at the top of quite a high bluff. I looked at the punctured trolley wheel and my heart sank. This was going to be a fair old effort to get to the campsite and given where I'd landed was clearly the beginning of a nature reserve, leaving the boat at the waterside was not on the cards. It took a major effort just to get the boat off the shingle and on to the footpath leading up the hill, and its incline was intimidatingly steep. I decided to walk up to the top and scope out what I was letting myself in for.

Half a mile – it felt a lot further – and ten minutes later, I reached the park entrance, where the volunteers firmly informed me that I shouldn't have landed in the reserve. I'd known the spit was off limits but had assumed that, as the campsite was where it was, the base of the bluff was all right. I was in a quandary: my muscles were feeling the paddle, even though it was only ten miles, and it would be a further fifteen to the other site I'd marked the night before, and to get back in was only doubling the faux pas I'd already made. I pointed out that I was already ashore, and we agreed that getting the boat up was probably the sensible option. I walked back down, steeled myself, and began the arduous task of dragging Minnie up the path.

To start with it was an absolute bugger. The path was what felt like one in six, and I could only manage five metres at a time. The punctured wheel was a nightmare, but I dread to think what it would have been like with no wheels at all. By the time I reached the relative flat of the top of the first turn I think I'd expended more energy than in the ten miles I'd paddled over the last two and a half hours, and I still had the majority of a still-uphill route to go. I think it was an hour before I reached the park entrance, and I was sweating like a glass blower's backside, even though my drysuit was off and safely stowed in the cockpit. For another breather, I walked the next half a mile to the campsite to ferret out the last of my route. It was another hour before I was setting up my hammock, a relief to be on the camp site, and I now had another problem to solve. Where could I get back on the water, and how much effort could it be? I knew there was a slip ramp three miles to the East, but with the wheel as it was… It was something I'd ponder for the next thirty-six hours.

First go at full-boat camping: Dungeness Campsite

I used the downtime I had the next day to get the tyre fixed with the camp supervisor and get an American sim for my phone. The latter entailed a seven mile walk into Sequim. When the footpath turned into roadworks near the centre of town, I was lucky enough to bump into Jay and Cheryl out walking their dogs, who very kindly drove me back to Dungeness, saving me a very hot, dry walk back. I also discovered during the night that it's easy to lose your bearings walking too far from the hammock for a pee in the dark, even with a torch. The trees on the campsite combined with the absence of ambient light made even finding the path back in the dark a challenge.

2022 : Final Practice Run – 23 Miles

Everything still looking very good at this point

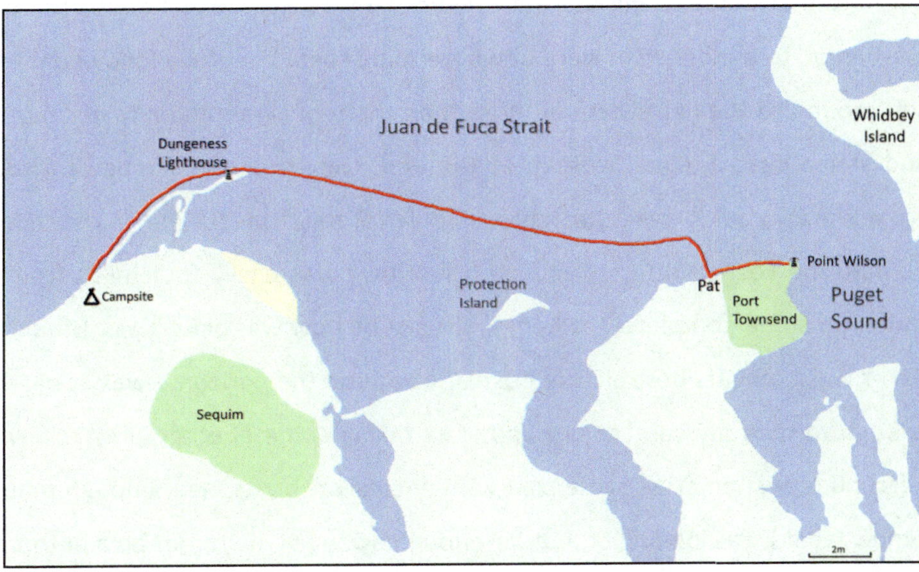

I struck camp on Tuesday morning, loading everything into the hatches, and then wheeled the boat to the top of the reserve. The same park volunteers were there, and they kindly steered me to a nearby park ranger. I wasn't about to get myself in a heap of bother by trying to sneak down. Had it come to it I'd have walked to the boat ramp all those miles away. Thankfully he said I was OK to go back to the base of the bluff, as long as I trundled the boat a further half a mile back down the beach to where the rock fall warning signs ended, and then stayed at least a hundred metres from shore. With his instructions ringing in my ears, I set off down the path. With the exception of the last steep slope, it was a piece of cake to get to the beach, and with the now reinflated tyre it was less of a struggle to get along the beach.

The forecast for the day was impeccable: no wind, with the tide changing in my favour from slack to a flow at around four o'clock. It was now close to one in the afternoon, and as I set off the sky was clear, and the waves I'd crashed on to the beach in were nowhere to be seen. I dutifully followed the spit around to the lighthouse at more than the requisite minimum distance and glided past the seal reserve at the end. Only one seal popped up to scope me out, but it was a start: first wildlife for the trip. The line on the GPS pointed me East-South-East and on a line that was easily four miles from shore, and I felt completely at home. The sea by now was plate glass. Mount Baker was doing its best picture postcard pose on the horizon. I was at ease enough to take my camera out and start taking some photographs. To my left a nuclear submarine came past with two escort boats, near enough that I knew what I was looking at, but far enough away for me to not be a bother to them. I did learn later that the escort boats would chase you away if they felt you got too close. I was in my element. I was paddling at an easy rate that I felt I could maintain all day. Minnie and my fitness were making the load she was carrying no burden to my strokes, and as four o'clock passed the tide gee-d me along even quicker. I'd homed in on the land mass which was almost certainly North Beach leading to Port Townsend, and I started to eat up the miles.

Protection Island was to my right. It took a couple of hours for it to shift past me, but I'd readied myself for this. In all the training on the Ashby, I'd never had more than five minutes before the next landmark appeared, either a river bend or a bridge. I knew from Lake Laberge in Yukon that the scenery was going to stay monotonously beautiful for hours at a time. So it was with

Protection Island. Even when I drew level, it took another hour to drift out of my vision, and it was about the time it disappeared that the coastguard began to pipe up on the VHF.

Three miles offshore and plate glass. Heading to Port Townsend

"Coastguard to white sea kayaker, coastguard to white sea kayaker: Are you in distress? Over."

Bear in mind this was my first ever communication on a VHF radio in the wild. How exciting! They're contacting a white sea kayaker too. I put two and two together and replied without really thinking it all through.

"Sea kayaker to coastguard. Sea kayaker to coastguard. I am not in distress."

And as an afterthought:

"Over"

There was silence for a few minutes. What was I thinking? Should I say more? The VHF sprung back into life.

"Coastguard to sea kayaker, coastguard to sea kayaker: Are you sure?"

"Sea kayaker to coastguard. Sea kayaker to coastguard. Yes, I'm sure."

Pause…

"Over."

It was quiet for a few more minutes, and then: ""Coastguard to sea kayaker, coastguard to sea kayaker: Do you have a phone on board?"

What was this? I had a radio, and they'd heard me, but you can't go at it with the coastguard, and I was guessing especially not the US ones if they were anything like US Customs.

Yes, I replied, I had a phone, but it was in the back of the boat and, the boat being a kayak, not really accessible at that moment.

Another five minutes passed, and the radio crackled into life again. "Please call us," they said. "Here's the number." I frantically tried to get into my map case to get the pen out, but the static from the pages effectively glued the case together, and they were mostly through giving me the number by the time my pen was out. It wasn't even a case of me agreeing to call back – I felt I had no choice they were that insistent, but in any case, I told them it would be at least fifteen minutes until I made shore and could reach the phone.

I was quite pissed off by this time, but as I said before: you can't go at it with the Coastguard. I was having to go off course, and my six o'clock arrival was going out of the window. I flew into North Beach, just remembered to haul up the rudder in time, stepped out and retrieved my phone from the day hatch. My luck was definitely out now, because I had no bars on the signal, not even one.

The beach wasn't devoid of people. A man with a bushy grey beard was walking towards me with his two dogs. "Do you need any help?" he asked. "Yes", I replied, "the coastguard seems to think I'm in distress, which I am clearly not, and I need to enlighten them to this, but I have no signal". He dug out his mobile, which thankfully was better connected than mine. We found the number for Port Townsend Coastguard, who redirected us to Seattle. I explained that, yes, I was a sea kayaker in a white boat, and I was ringing to clear up the misunderstanding we'd had over the last half an hour. The officer at the other end of the line explained that they had had a report of a white sea kayak capsizing off Whidbey Island. I'd missed this detail in earlier transmissions, or it hadn't been relayed - I suspect the former had occurred, as Whidbey was well to the East of where I was. Apparently, my radio had mostly come across as static, hence the requirement for the confirmatory phone call. I told him that, while there may well have been a capsize, it wasn't me, and the conversation ended the whole episode in amicable fashion.

I thanked the guy with the grey beard for his help. It was a relief to have cleared things up. We got a selfie of the pair of us on the beach, with the sea in the background. He asked me where I was headed.

"Round to Port Townsend," I replied.

You could see in that moment a lightbulb blink on over his head:

"Are you in the race?"

Well, yes, this was my last training run, and I was enjoying Juan de Fuca, at least until the coastguard had shattered the calm.

"Where are you staying?"

Well, I was planning on stopping at the Fort Worden Campground.

"Do you want to stop at my place?"

Whoa... I'd half expected the hospitality I'd had from Ian in Victoria, but this was a real shock. The independent part of my brain was saying no, I'd planned to camp, so stick to the plan. However, the other part of my brain was saying that I'd never get another chance like this. "You know what?" I said, "I'd love that, if that's OK".

Meeting Patrick for the first time. North Beach, Port Townsend

Grey Beard introduced himself as Patrick Johnson. He'd have to get the dogs home first, and in any case getting the boat up the bluff would be hard. After my experience at Dungeness two days earlier, and even with wheels that were now both fully inflated, I was not in a rush to repeat a hefty hauling operation. We agreed that I'd paddle on to Point Wilson and he'd meet me there. This was beyond bloody brilliant.

It took another hour to get into Point Wilson. Again, I misjudged where to land, and found myself with a no-go nature reserve between me and the car park. Even with my Ikea bags, which I use to corral all my gear into manageable carrying units, it took an extra twenty minutes and several shuttles, including dragging the boat a couple of hundred yards in the water, to relocate the gear I'd unloaded into the car park. As I got the first bag to the bench near the lighthouse a clapped-out orange beetle bumbled in. The lady driving it yelled over to check I was Bob, then that she was Patrick's wife, Peg, and Patrick had managed to lose one of the dogs coming back, but that he'd be along for me soon. Not a problem. As she disappeared, I moved the rest of my gear and the boat away from the beach, and I'd just changed when Patrick arrived.

It's an odd feeling deviating from your intended plans at the best of times. Normally it's because something has gone wrong, and very rarely because something has gone right-er. This was weird in the most brilliant way possible. We loaded the boat on the roof, and all the dry bags, stacked the Ikea bags in the boot, and headed off to... well, Patrick's place. He gave me a bit of a guided tour to Port Townsend as we went, seeing the town's deer herd at the side of the road, and passing a lake. At Patrick's we unloaded everything into the garage and stepped inside.

I'd more than landed on my feet. Patrick and Peg are two of the most generous souls you could hope to meet. It turned out Patrick was a volunteer with the race, and absolutely passionate about it. You couldn't fail but warm to them both. That evening we sat down and ate and talked until late into the night. I couldn't quite believe it, but they were to be my hosts, help, and introduction to Port Townsend over the next few days. As I went to bed that night, I was in a state of disbelief and just overwhelmingly happy. I would, I am sure, have managed at Fort Worden campsite, but this? The weather forecast for the foreseeable was a repeat of that day, calm, and on the back of a successful paddle from Dungeness Spit I was feeling upbeat. Most of all, I was here in Port Townsend, at the start.

The following day Patrick took me to the Northwest Maritime Centre, the home of R2AK. I wasn't sure what to expect but the place blew me away. I'd been so intent on the race that the Centre's wider purposes had completely washed over me. Here was an educational establishment – with loads of classrooms – to teach people about maritime life. There's a huge workshop, with boats all over the place, and if I am correct, in the middle of it, a Pocock boat. I am a huge fan of "The Boys in the Boat", and the realisation that here I was, in Joe Rantz territory, just added to the excitement. There was already at least one R2AK boat out the front of the centre, an Angus Row Cruiser, a twenty-odd-foot sailboat that was only marginally larger – by width – than my kayak. No racers to be seen, yet.

Patrick took me up to meet Daniel and Jake, Race to Alaska's big cheeses. It was like waiting for a job interview as we sat outside the offices in the main part of the centre. Again, it was surreal meeting these people you'd seen on film and met in print over the last half a decade. Patrick filled Daniel in on our serendipitous meeting on the beach the day before, and beyond that, it's a blur what we discussed. I'd toyed with bringing them Harris tweed waistcoats in view of the write-up they'd done me over with, or some Marmite, but there'd been no space in my bags.

Carbo-loading was de rigueur, so Patrick took me to Tommyknockers, where we both polished off a mac and cheese. This was to become my lunchtime haunt and something of a routine for the next few days. I was left to enjoy the town and pick up yet more missing kit that afternoon. I was still short of a boat repair kit, and I could have done with better storage for the flares, but I was unable to find what I was looking for. The rest of the day was more hospitality: a trip to a music recital, walks with the dogs, and generally taking a breath after what I'd completed, and before what was to come.

By Thursday the weather forecast was worryingly shifting. The plate glass, wind-free expectations I had from paddling round from Dungeness on Tuesday were replaced by a front moving in, bringing with it the portent of force six winds. With my relative inexperience of the sea, this felt like my worst fears were being realised. The likelihood of needing all of the thirty six hours I had available to get to Victoria was escalating, and the alternate routes I had planned were coming to the forefront of the options I might have to take. By now I was even contemplating a three-kilometre portage across Whidbey Island to get into its lee.

It was only when Helen and Steve arrived on Friday morning that I realised just how high the needle had risen on my tensionometer. Pat and Peg were wonderful, and I don't know how I would have managed without their help in Port Townsend, but when Helen stepped through their door and gave me a hug, she just hit the release button on the pressure. I could now feel just how strained I was about the impending crossing. It wasn't my ability to get to Victoria. It was the sure-fire knowledge that, if the conditions remained bad, my whole venture was in jeopardy. In addition to being family, one of the other great things about Helen is that she is bossy, in a totally "let's get organised" sort of way, and right at this moment having her there was just the tonic I required.

In the middle of the excitement of their arrival I had a call from Paula Hunt, a journalist who'd been emailing me and trying to get hold of me ever since she'd stumbled across the picture of "Please don't die" cakes posted on the Zen Dog feed. We'd met a photographer who knew her at the Northwest Maritime Centre while waiting to see Jake and Daniel, but our timings had been woefully out. It wasn't that I was unhappy to talk to journalists; it was simply that there was so much going on that was higher in my priority list. We snatched a quick Q and A as I tried hopelessly to multitask at getting sorted out with Helen, Steve, and the boat.

Helen and Steve had brought with them my food supplies for the entire race, all twenty-one kilos of it, and its bulk was equal cause for concern. It had been hard enough packing Minnie for the short trip to Port Townsend. Helen had packed the food into day bags, each containing a breakfast bar, and a multitude of Clif, breakfast, nut butter, muesli, and chocolate bars. We spent the morning getting these and everything else – camping and paddling gear - into dry sacks. Each dry sack then got labelled – anything to make finding the right piece of kit easier. We then spent some time fitting all the bags into the hatches. This was packing bordering on requiring a Masters or even a Doctorate in n-dimensional physics. The little bags needed to be in the further reaches of the compartments and therefore had to contain the gear that was in less demand, like the spare spraydeck. At the same time, I had to be able to get them out if I needed them, and on my first pack it became clear that, without a line attached to the bag, they were nigh-on impossible to recover.

As we packed, I made a diagram on the back of one of my maps of where everything was. Steve then produced a stopwatch, and I unpacked and repacked the boat until I was reasonably comfortable with the process and the time it took. I'd had to resort to using a deck bag for some of the food, and there were now day packs of food in all of the compartments, something I'd been keen to avoid for bear reasons. Still, we reasoned that as I got to the second week of the trip, the food supplies would dwindle, and I'd not only be able to lose the bag from the front deck, but I'd be able to re-jig all of the food into the front hatch.

I had organised a meet-up with Bill Hay that lunchtime, an old family friend, the husband of my godmother, and a resident of Tacoma - a town a couple of hours away from Port Townsend. Bill had got in touch a couple of months before, alerted by my mother that I'd be in the vicinity. He'd been hoodwinked by my race bio ("I gather you're a bit of a royalist"), but he was looking forward to having an excuse to get his Jaguar F-Type out for a spin and check in with me. I was aware that he was not well and that he was undergoing chemotherapy for stage four cancer. Nevertheless, it was a shock to see him when he arrived, after he'd had had treatment that morning,. If ever there was a reminder of why things like R2AK should be done, Bill was it. That said, it was a huge delight and boon to see him and share a couple of hours with him that Friday, and the moment he pulled up in the F-Type was priceless. The boats taking part in the pace were all head-turners, but the effect of that car on passers-by outside of the Northwest Maritime Centre was quite something else!

There was little left to do with the boat now fully packed and there was not much to be done with the weather forecast. Helen and Steve distracted me for most of Saturday with a drive out into the Olympic National Park and up Mount Olympus. I can't have been good company with everything locked in on the Monday, but it was good to be away for a day.

That evening they dropped me off in town with Ian and Janice, and they took me up to the racers' hog roast over at Jake's place. The roast is a chance for all the participants to get together before the race and meet the opposition. It was a hell of a spread that Jake had laid on for everyone. For me, it felt like being the plus one of a friend at a wedding, where the only person you know is the mate you went with, that "mate" being Ian and Janice. As one of the two kayak teams amongst a large group of sailors – Ian and Janice being the other team – I had less in common with the other teams, and to my discredit I hadn't really read many of the bios of this year's participants. Ian and Janice introduced me properly to Doug Shoop and James Gibling, both Angus Row Cruiser sailors. The Angus boats aren't that much bigger than Minnie, and these guys looked like they were going to spend as much time with oars as with sail, but I still felt like the littlest guy at the party.

I picked out the French crew, Nathalie and Boris from Loustic Supersonic, and played the European solidarity card, striking up a conversation in Franglais. They'd not long picked up their boat; the pedal drive system wasn't engaging as it should and there was still a raft of work for them to do. They'd figured with the forecast that they'd have time once they got through leg one and arrived in Victoria to fix it. One of the Kootenay Paddlewheelers was sat to my other side, and we exchanged pleasantries about our expectations. There's a point at which stays and sheets don't quite tie up with spraydecks, but it was fascinating to see how different a race experience they were going to have. The Kootenays were contenders to win the race, and were contemplating taking the "Outside", heading up the West Coast of Vancouver Island. While their decision wasn't yet made, or at least not yet publicised, their challenges were clearly going to be very different and more concentratedly intense than mine, not least as they wouldn't hit land after Victoria until the finish.

The Saturday night hog roast was the real lock-in to the R2AK agenda, and Sunday saw everything properly begin to count down. That began with the boat inspection first thing. We loaded Minnie up and drove her to the Northwest Maritime Centre, setting her down next to Don't Tell Mom's rowboat. My pre-race inspector, Martin Musson, turned out to be a Brit, and a Brit who had also completed the race. VHF? Check. Flares? Check. Compass and navigation gear? EPIRB? Check. Check... I was through fairly fast, and additionally gave him the links for my SPOT tracker. Being the trusting soul that I am of tracking devices, I was more comfortable with the idea of taking two units just in case one didn't work. This turned out to be a strikingly good approach over the next two weeks. I picked up my official race tracker, and my race t-shirt. Checks were passed.

There were plenty of racers, past and present, milling around the grass bank by the start. Dameon and Leigh, who had rowed as Backwards AF in 2019 were there. Leigh was racing with her sister, Clare, as "Don't Tell Mom". Dameon, as he said when I asked him, was doing the sensible thing and working instead of racing, although it was abundantly clear that he was itching to be back in the boat. Christina from team Solveig was there. I'd already met Katie Stewart earlier in the week, a conversation that rather disintegrated after thirty seconds as I realised that she understandably hadn't a clue I was a racer. As "who the hell are you" moments go, it was comical, and easier to leave her to the more important preparation of her row cruiser. As a tracker junkie who'd followed all the previous races, and who had repeatedly watched their videos through lockdown as an antidote to not being able to race, this was hobnobbing with R2AK royalty.

I spotted Karl Kruger near the registration area and went over. His boat, Team Skywalker, hadn't made the start. He explained that the complexity of the control systems design and the time constraints had meant that it was not tried and tested enough to risk the route. Given the all-consuming question arising from the weather, I put it to him: "What would you do?" Karl started talking, a steady train of thought articulated, reasoned, and evidenced as he went. Out came the "Windy" app on his phone, and he went through the forecast, the wind strengths, directions. Tide information along with flows through the Gulf Islands. Factoring in the time constraints, he ran over the direct route and went to further options, supporting his rationales with more information from other apps. You could paddle beyond Port Angeles, and then use the prevailing winds and tide to manage a reverse ferry over Juan de Fuca on an incoming tide. There was a possibility that, instead of aiming for Victoria from Dungeness, aim for San Juan Island and paddle round to its East in the lee, coming back down past Oak Bay. There was the possibility I'd already considered of crossing Whidbey Island, and then using the San Juan's as a shelter to cross the border. Karl gave his time freely and generously; I think not having a clue who I was. That he covered some of my plans was reassuring, but that he came up with plans E, F, G, and H to supplement my plans A to D was quite something. To anyone else, all these options might have seemed like lunacy, but this was Karl. You just figured that if he had to implement any one of the options he was suggesting, he'd deliver on it, not only completing the route on his SUP, but completing it within the thirty-six hours. The biggest worry was that all of these required covering the best part of eighty miles, when crow's distance was forty, yet here was the spirit of R2AK personified, an elite and the best of sportsmen. It didn't diminish the problem of the impending storm though. It was coming, plans or no plans.

Helen and Steve were doing their best to get me to load calories with breakfasts, mid-morning snacks, and burgers. They were both sporting my team T-shirts with "Zen" on the front and "...and Zen again..." on the back, with the respective dates of legs one and two underneath. As we caught some more calories in a café near the start, Helen was asked by another customer how on earth she'd managed to get today's date on the shirts. We left, slightly bemused, as not only had they missed the point of the t-shirts, but they'd fluffed the date by a day.

Back at the starting area "show and tell" with the boats was in full swing. We'd been asked to put the boats on show after the inspections, and if possible, to be on hand to answer questions. There was plenty of interest, questions ranging from "you're doing it in that?" to how everything fit in the boat, and how many miles a day I was hoping to do. On the latter I didn't have a clue. I knew what I was capable of on flat inland water, but I had no idea what my daily routine would end up being. It was genuinely a pleasure to be able to answer questions, although I still felt like an impostor next to some of the other crews, and being the littlest boat, I think I had every right to feel the smallest.

Around lunchtime, old racing friends Bob and Toni showed up, having driven over from Sequim a couple of hours away. The last time I'd seen them was when we'd shared a table with them at the Yukon River Quest banquet in 2016, and cheered Bob as he got his finishers pin. Races form special bonds between people, and Bob and Toni fit that category. I felt, along with the friends I'd made in Port Townsend, and especially from Helen and Steve, that a lot of people had my back.

Three o'clock was race briefing time, so we headed up to the main room in the Maritime Centre. I cannot for the life of me remember who I sat with for the briefing, but the delivery was everything I expected from what I'd seen of Jake and Daniel in the race film, and also from all of the information in the race packet. There were additional nuggets, like the use of channel 68 for race radio the following morning. Yet all the while the briefing went on there was the nagging concern about the thirty-six-hour race window. My plan was to grab Ian and Janice afterward and try and form a race alliance. It had worked in the Yukon, and with the conditions here it seemed a reasonable safety tack to exploit again.

As everyone filed out of the room, I collared the pair of them. They introduced me to Drew, team Arm and Leg, who had just completed the Seventy Forty-Eight the day before in his solo sea kayak. The Seventy Forty-Eight is like a taster for the R2AK, yet a race in its own right from Tacoma down to Port Townsend. It's a contest for human powered craft, and there are some who compete in that, and then either go on to compete in R2AK or to complete leg one to Victoria. Drew was the latter and all four of us were worried.

We accosted Daniel. Drew, Ian, and Janice very eloquently put across our concerns. I'd like to say I contributed, but I stood at the side like the dumb English idiot I am and just made up the numbers. The concerns ran largely as follows: if the race were to go ahead with the time constraint of thirty-six hours in place, there were two possible outcomes for the smaller and human-powered crews. The first was that the sensible participants amongst us would factor in all of the existing weather conditions, make the correct safety decision, sit out the storm in Port Townsend, and be disqualified for not arriving within the time limit. The second was that there might be some among us who, having invested a lot of time, energy, effort, and money in getting to the start, would take the foolhardy option and go for it, and damned be the consequences, and those consequences could be fatal. I was fairly sure I'd be in the first bracket, but not entirely convinced that the stubborn gene wouldn't kick in before the following morning and move me into the second. I was tempted to weigh in with the further argument of the chances of more British kayakers looking at a race scuppered by the risk of this sort of elimination but decided against it. Daniel is no fool, and to his credit he listened to what our small group had to say. He made no promises but told us he would consider what we'd put to him. The four of us then agreed that the course of action we were likely to take at five am the next day was to paddle over the start line, as required to avoid an even earlier disqualification, pull into the beach, and sit out to Tuesday and hope for better conditions.

On the way out I bumped into Interstice's Lilian, who had also just completed the Seventy Forty-Eight. Again, we shared the gale concerns. She was contemplating the Whidbey Island option as well, except she was thinking about rowing around the South of the island rather than portaging over, which would have given her three figure mileage to Victoria, something I think would have pushed me to breaking point way too early in the venture. At this point I asked her if she'd consider heading up to

Ketchikan if we did get eliminated from the official race. I'd come too far not to try and paddle the Inside Passage. We agreed, and I think I roped in Ian and Janice too, that a "Not the R2AK" would be on the cards if it all went belly up.

There was also a treat on the way out. A lovely lady, Melanie Rice, had prepared sweetie bags for every R2AK entrant. There was a mound of sweetie bags just outside of the meeting hall, each one labelled with a contestant's name, one bag for each of us. Ian had already told me that Melanie had a soft spot for the human powered teams. I collected my bag, as did Ian, although he supplemented his with the extras that Melanie offered. I wished later that I'd done the same!

There wasn't much left that we could do at the start, so I left Minnie safely tucked up next to Don't tell Mom's boat, and Helen and Steve took me back to Pat and Peg's place. As we sat down, Helen picked up a race update from HQ. Daniel had indeed taken on board our concerns. The race window for the first leg had been increased by a day. The forecast from Tuesday night was a major improvement. The release was immediate. It actually looked like we had a chance after all!

Patrick had a copy of the Peninsula Daily News containing Paula Hunt's article on the race. It covered several crews taking part in the race: Dark Star, Lilian's Interstice, Rite of Passage, and me. To my amusement the piece was propped up by the picture of Kate's cakes.

> *Bob McCall, 52, has been kayaking since he was 14 years old, but said he felt a "slight bit of trepidation" ahead of the upcoming race. McCall, from Sharnford, England, had been looking forward to taking part in R2AK back in 2020;*

he even had a kayak built in Canada in anticipation of competing. Three years later, McCall was finally able to retrieve it from Team Oaracle, a Victoria, B.C. kayak team, that had generously stored it for him.

He finally got to see his 18-foot kayak a week ago and first put it into the water on Sunday – one week before the start of the race – and has been training ever since.

"She's a beaut," McCall said. "She'll do fine."

Although an experienced ultra kayak racer, McCall said he had never paddled the kind of open water he will have to navigate in the R2AK. His coworkers at MIRA (Motor Industry Research Association) gave him a good-natured send-off with a package of cupcakes labelled "Please don't die."

"There are limits to insanity," McCall said.

(Paula Hunt : Excerpt from "Adventurers gearing up for Race to Alaska run", Peninsula Daily News June 11-12, 2022)

It was strange to be in the article, and stranger still to realise what I'd come out with. I hoped at least that work would forgive me for the Motor industry Research Association bit. MIRA hasn't been called that for nearly three decades, and it's actively discouraged.

Within an hour there was an email from Drew. He was co-ordinating a hook-up between himself, me and Oaracle for the first leg. Between email exchanges and phone calls we managed the skeleton of a plan. As per the

"Paddle over the start line and stop" plan we'd already agreed, we would wait it out for at least a day in Port Townsend and then see if Tuesday was better. The idea of being in a small flotilla was such a relief. We had an alliance of sorts. As I went to bed that night the stress had diminished, and with the help of a Tylenol night-time sleeping pill, I zonked out a lot happier than I otherwise would have been.

13 June -The Proving Ground

Day One: Port Townsend to Dungeness Lighthouse – 21 Miles

Everything is go.

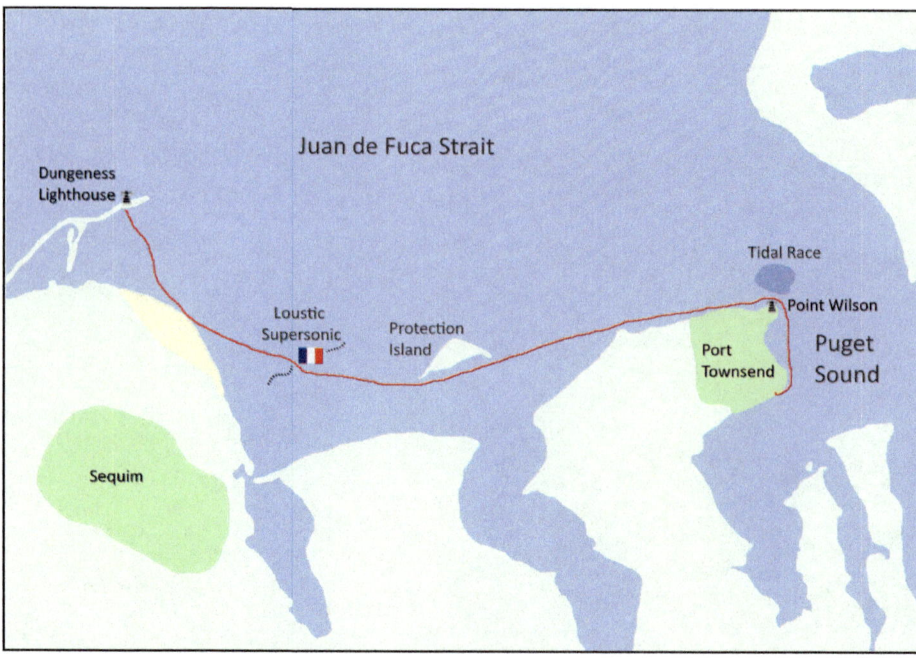

I didn't need the three am alarm after all. The nerves or the anticipation of what was coming had me awake twenty minutes shy of it triggering, and I was up and changed into my race gear by the time it pinged. I stowed what little was left of my gear in the dry sacks I'd left out, day clothes in the main clothes bag, the phones in the electricals bag, both passport and wallet in the "close to hand" sack. Patrick, I think, was already up and ready for his race volunteer duties for that morning. With Minnie already in situ at the start, there were only the Ikea bags full of the dry sacks to load. With the plan to moor up for the day, there was no real pressure on me for the start. I had sixty hours now, not thirty-six to make Victoria, and I had Oaracle and Arm and Leg for company. I'd be seeing Pat and Peg later in the morning too.

We arrived at the start by four. The weather was holding. The wind was not too strong, and it wasn't raining. We loaded Minnie under torchlight. I was comfortable with the order and location of each bag by now. The open Ikea bag contents in the back and day hatch, the closed one with food and clothes in the front. True to form, Helen insisted I pack them alone for practice.

By four thirty it was time to get on the water. All of team Zen Dog were there, Patrick, Peg, Steve, and Helen, enough to lift about one hundred kilos of boat – at least it felt that heavy – down to the water's edge. I had filled both dromedary bags with water, one stowed in the day hatch, the other clipped down between my legs in the cockpit in front of the seat. It made getting in awkward, but it ballasted the centre of the boat well enough. Farewells were not really on the agenda given the plan to pull in again within the hour. I put on my brown paddling hat and pulled out into the assembling armada.

Crowds were growing on the pier. I circled round, getting used to the feel of the laden boat. There was the odd "good luck" exchanged with other crews. I sought out Ian and Janice, who launched shortly before five, and Drew. The sky was beginning to turn a cloudy blue when the race started. There had been some debate over what was going to be played to serenade us over the start line. Race tradition up until that point had been to broadcast the strains of the Russian national anthem, but with geopolitical events underway in Europe that wasn't on the cards. I didn't register that it was the Ukrainian anthem that saw us off. I do recall the sheer disbelief after the disappointment of the last two years, and the tribulations of COVID and trials of lockdown, that it was finally happening.

As we passed the crowd on the pier, Drew pulled in immediately to take his kids to school, the benefit and drawback, I guess, of living locally. I was close to Oaracle when Janice turned to me and said:

"It doesn't look too bad. How about we paddle down to Wilson's Point and take a look round the corner?"

Whoa! This wasn't in the script! I started to process what this meant. I knew in that instant, deep down, that going to the point meant going round the point, and out on to the edge of Juan de Fuca. More importantly to me, Drew wasn't here now, and we'd agreed that we three teams were going to paddle as one. If I went with Ian and Janice, I'd be reneging on an agreement with Drew. Although I didn't know him from Adam, a deal was a deal, and I felt shoddy about the idea of reneging on it. I had, in that instant, to weigh it up against the bare fact that I knew Ian and Janice *just slightly* better. They'd helped me. Lots, both before the race while I was four thousand miles away, and again massively in Victoria. I wasn't really factoring in the weather here, more who I felt comfortable paddling with, and I'd share the judgement on that at Wilson's, and again I knew what that decision was going to be. I'd have to throw all of my eggs, my boat, and myself into one basket, and the best and most selfish option was with Oaracle. It had to be a quick decision, and I think if I had to make it again it would be the same one. With Ian and Janice it was, and off we went.

I was glad I'd set the boat up for a full paddle, with the water hose feeding out of the cockpit in the right place and food on the decks. There would be no farewells to my pit crew, who were by now probably wondering what the hell was going on. We paddled down to the point in relative comfort, no real waves, and not bucketloads of wind. The bigger craft, which was everybody else, were either immediately ahead of us or barrelling past us to the point. I was still pinching myself. I felt disconnected from what I was actually doing, almost in denial of the race being underway.

The water from Puget Sound flows on the ebb around Wilson's Point and out into Juan de Fuca Strait. From the lighthouse there is a narrow stretch of water, maybe a couple of hundred metres wide, between the Point and a tidal race. Beyond this the sea water is in full drainage mode over the shallows when the tide is on the ebb, and beyond that there are millions of tonnes of water moving rapidly out towards the Pacific. That day, combined with the ever-increasing wind, we knew the conditions were going to be fairly biblical out there. As we arrived at Wilson's, Janice got a message through on the VHF that my SPOT tracker wasn't working. Oaracle pulled alongside and she reset it for me, a sign of how little I trusted letting go of the paddles at that moment. Then we edged around the corner in that calm stretch of water and headed West.

We were fully aware that most of the other crews had headed out beyond that tidal race and into the strait. We listened to the drama that is Race to Alaska unfold on our VHFs over the next two hours, as we headed for

Protection Island. It was sobering and terrifying in equal measure. Wind against tide generates some spectacular sea conditions, and several teams got caught out. We could hear snatches of rescues "out there". It was like when you are watching a horror movie, where you know something gruesome is taking place just off screen. The butcher's bill accounted for some very experienced sailors. We were later to read about B-Team's capsize and Narwhal's dismasting, but it was Razzle Dazzle's flip, bow over stern, that was the most epically breathtaking. It confirmed for us little guys that Plan A, the home run directly to Victoria that day, would have been nigh-on suicidal.

Dawn on Day One with Oaracle off North Beach. The carnage was to the East. Courtesy of Helen Green

Hugging the coast was all attention consuming as it was. The waves were mercifully head-on, meaning there was no nausea inducing side swells to deal with. We could hear shouts from the shore as we passed North Beach where I'd met Patrick. Helen and Steve had come down to cheer us on, the last time I'd see them for a while. Oaracle was seemingly effortlessly pulling ahead, and I was paddling at a higher effort percentage than I'd have liked just to keep up. In an ideal scenario I would have been chugging along at around fifty percent effort, but here I was fearful of losing them. As we neared Protection Island, staying sensibly to the South and as far from trouble as possible, I cut corners to keep up. I'd like to claim that they were faster as their boat was lighter and there were two of them, but the reality was I couldn't hold a candle to their paddling ability.

It was when we got to the Western end of Protection Island that I got a chance to steal a bit of a march on them. To be clear, this was not "Competitive Bob" in action, but the Bob who wanted to keep as close to another boat as possible given the conditions. Ian and Janice stopped for a tracker check and a bit to eat, so I rounded the rocky, sandy spit on the end of the island, took a bearing on what I reckoned to be the South end of Dungeness Spit, and paddled on.

When you make a decision or a mistake on the sea, the sea doesn't let you know the ramifications of that choice for a while afterwards. Twenty minutes later, the water was getting decidedly undulating, and the tops of the swells were high enough that I was losing sight of land when I was in the troughs. I was looking around for Oaracle, now worried that they had made a beeline for the nearest shore rather than heading in the same direction as me. When I say looking around, I was snatching glances whenever I felt there was a spare nanosecond when I didn't have to concentrate on the swells. I started to question my choice. There was no panic, just the consideration of a course correction to head more towards the shore than my crow-flies bearing. For now, I had to suck it up.

Half an hour on I spotted a sail. It was Boris and Nathalie, the French Loustic crew. I overtook them. There was a wave and a shouted greeting lost in the noise of the wind, but I actually overtook them! I accosted them about this long after. How the hell does a kayak overtake a sailboat in that wind?

“Ohhhh.” came the reply from Nathalie. “We wurr zeeenkeeng!”

It transpired that the top section of the boat had managed to detach itself from the hull, and they were shipping water at a potentially race- and boat-ending rate. They were limping towards Sequim to get it repaired in more conducive conditions, from where they would make the most of the extra twenty-four hours to squeeze into Victoria in time for the second leg.

Oaracle reappeared, much to my relief, and steamed on past. None of us wanted to be out in these conditions any longer than we needed to be. Neither crew had stated it, but we both knew that our target was the lighthouse at the end of the spit. In 2019, when the conditions had also been bad – maybe not as bad as this – human-powered crews had congregated there to wait out the bad weather and narrow the main crossing. Aside from Lilian’s publicised being denied a camping spot there while practising, it made sense to follow these tactics. The further we got away from Protection Island, the further Ian and Janice moved away from me. We were both playing it safer though by cutting in towards the mainland.

This brought its own problems. The tide was now well and truly ebbed out, and as I drew close to the shore, I hit a mix of a kelp and reed bed. With almost every stroke I was getting the paddles tangled up in weed or lifting kelp out of the water. It was energy-sapping, and I got more and more wound up. I was almost inside the Spit line now, and I could see the lighthouse off to my right, but the frustration got the better of me. I pulled into the shore and clambered out of the boat. There followed about five minutes of swearing at nobody and everything as I let rip at myself for stopping, for the wind, for losing Ian and Janice, for getting stuck in the weeds, and just generally not being good enough. I grabbed some food from the deck and made the most of not having to contend with the waves as I demolished a couple of nut butter bars. I re-embarked, only to find that the rudder had started to play silly buggers and wouldn't shift. On pulling in again I discovered that Minnie had a cleat just under the rudder line which had done what it was supposed to do: cleated the line in situ, just the wrong situ. You have to remember that, for all the paddling I'd done, this was only the third time I'd ever paddled Minnie. I uncleated it, set off, and made probably the most impetuous decision of the whole trip. I set my sights on Dungeness lighthouse.

Dungeness Spit is a five-mile-long bar that sticks out into Juan de Fuca Strait. I'd already paddled its outside on the way to Port Townsend and was bloody glad I wasn't out there today. The spit and the sheltered bay on its inside is a nature reserve, and at the end of the spit, beyond the lighthouse, is a seal sanctuary. I had already been regaled with stories of the epic eddies at the end of the spit and had no intention of going anywhere near those. I could see the lighthouse, and I knew to get there would be the ferry glide to end all ferry glides.

A ferry glide involves facing a boat, usually into the current, offsetting at one or two o'clock from the direction that current is coming from, and letting it push you crab-wise to your destination. Today it wasn't current I was contending with, but wind. Thirty to forty consistent knots of wind. I was to look this up on the Beaufort Scale long after I'd finished to find I'd been paddling in the wind equivalent of a force six to eight, and it doesn't take a genius to recognise tackling this crossing in those conditions was bonkers.

I got as level with the lighthouse as I thought I could, got well clear of the weed and kelp bed, and began to crab right and out into the open water. The waves were my own infinite rollercoaster. I was riding Minnie over the top of one wave, and then crashing through the next, repeating the cycle over and over. It was about three miles as the crow flies from where I re-embarked to my destination, but I was aiming at about twelve-thirty on my notional clock. As time wore on, I could see the lighthouse keeper's cottage downwind of the lighthouse, and in between was a very windswept tree. I was able to triangulate using these three landmarks and work out whether I was moving upwind of my destination or slipping towards the end of the spit. From that I could adjust my bearing accordingly.

After about two hours of traversing, I could feel I was slipping backwards. I realised that there was the distinct chance of missing the end of the spit. What then? I'd could end up in Juan de Fuca Strait, which was beyond contemplation. I knew if that happened, I'd have to turn tail and paddle either South to Sequim sideways over the waves, or all the way back, all twenty plus miles, to the start. I redoubled my efforts. Jump a wave. Crash through the next.

The spray deck wasn't keeping out the water either. My legs were sloshing around in the cockpit, and I had the weird sensation of being sat in a drysuit and feeling the water on my legs. Yet, for all of this, I never felt insecure in Minnie, never felt in danger of capsizing, and felt completely comfortable in my paddling ability and fitness for the race. I was taking a face full of water with every wave, and I was grateful for the retainer strap on my hat.

Nine hours from the start, and three hours from leaving land, I made it to the lighthouse. Ian and Janice came down, pointed me to the correct landing point between the yellow poles, and helped me and Minnie from the sea. My hat was white with the salt sprayed on to it from the whitecaps. We set Minnie down on the driftwood above the tide line. I was spent. I reckon that nine hours on a good day would have seen me to Victoria, and I'd made all of twenty miles. Yet there was a sense of relief and achievement of making it here.

The salt on the hat tells the tale... Dungeness Lighthouse, end of Day One

I immediately began to process what had happened. These were by far the worst conditions I'd ever taken on in a kayak, and I'd made it as far as any of the human-powered crew that day. The absence of space for fear vanished the moment I hit land, and it was not lost on me that, in crossing to the lighthouse, I'd done something reckless, impetuous, and probably beyond the limits of what I should have tried. The overarching thought pounding through my head at this point was, if the rest of the race bore any resemblance to the last half a day, I would be in deep, deep trouble.

Interlude : Dungeness Refuge

It looks beautiful from here.

Dungeness Lighthouse

I grabbed dry clothes, set out my kit to dry in the wind on the boat, strapped down under the bungees, picked up a day bag of food from my deck bag, and walked up to the lighthouse. It was a stunning nineteenth century wooden building, with outbuildings on one side and the keepers house across a beautifully maintained lawn to the other. The lawn, and the tree in the middle of it, looked totally incongruous out here in what felt like the middle of the sea.

I sat down to eat. Well, I slumped back on the lawn for a bit and just tried to get my breath back first. Others were there too. Leigh and Clare, Michelle and Carling, and a guy called Ken who was rowing the first leg. Ian and Janice outlined the current situation to me as I started to pile in food to re-energise. They had paddled around the inside of the spit, hugging closer to the shore, not taking the more impetuous route straight across. I think the others had taken more direct and rougher paths beyond Protection Island, riding the bronco but cutting the time to make it to our refuge. The lighthouse keepers were saying that we were unable to camp on the spit, the same scenario Lilian had found herself in a couple of months before. At the same time, the coastguard was telling the R2AK organisers and us that there was no way we were to be allowed to re-embark until Wednesday because of the conditions. We were stuck, and these groups, the lighthouse association, the nature reserve body, the race organisers, and the coastguard were brainstorming a solution. There was some discussion about slinging tarpaulins over the picnic benches on the lawn and sleeping underneath, which would have been very cosy in a sardine-like way. For now, we were just to wait while decisions were reached, and there was nothing to do but eat and talk.

The lighthouse is run by volunteers. To volunteer you can sign up to the eighteen-month-long waiting list and pay something like a thousand bucks for the privilege of being lighthouse keeper for a week. Being a lighthouse keeper involved a combination of being handyman, tour guide, cleaner, groundsman, and general dogsbody. This week was the turn of Bob, Blaine, Chip and company, and that afternoon I think it was Blaine who donned the tour guide hat and, one at a time under his supervision, we were able to ascend the lighthouse and look out over the strait. With whitecaps on all sides, I was relieved to be in here and not out there. As part of the tour, we got shown a replacement bulb for the beacon. If you were expecting an oversized one, you'd be disappointed; it was smaller than my little finger. It made the refracting design of the hood it went in all the more impressive.

The Dungeness Keepers.

Later we gathered for the keepers to relay the agreement reached as to what we were to do. There would be no departures until Wednesday morning, and then only subject to approval from the coastguard. We weren't allowed to camp on the lawn, but we could sleep in the museum on the ground floor of the lighthouse, so long as we promised not to go up the spiral staircase to the light. There were to be no fires, no flames of any kind, because of the risk to the wooden buildings. To allow us to eat, they would supply us with hot water so we could rehydrate our food. I don't think any of us could believe our luck. Meanwhile, an urn of hot water and a jug of fresh coffee appeared from the keepers, along with some freshly baked cookies and some sweets. We had properly fallen on our feet! We were safe and, to boot, we were going to be in the warm and dry for two nights instead of being out in the elements.

We schlepped back down to our boats, gathered sleeping bags and mats, and installed ourselves in the rooms. I got what appeared to be the keeper's old office, and I rolled out my kit under the stars and stripes hanging on the wall. Ian and Janice took the adjacent room, Carling and Michelle on the far side, and Leigh and Clare took the stairwell. Ken decided to sleep down with his rowboat by the logs. He was quite a distant character. I have no idea in the order of things when he'd arrived, but he'd rowed the slightest craft of all of us to the spit, and apparently with no drysuit, a very brave man.

When we bedded down for the night, I slept fitfully. No doubt the adrenaline from the day and the euphoria of being in the race contributed to my insomnia, but amusingly so did Ian's snores from the room next door.

Two nights at the museum. Luxury accommodation with snores.

Waking up that Tuesday morning in the knowledge that there was no opportunity to paddle to Victoria was a blessing. It was still windy but there was no rain, and once we'd had breakfast, we all mucked in on the keepers' chores. First up was repairing the paths. Each path through the scrub was marked by driftwood lining the edges. Over time much of this had rotted away and needed replacement from the plentiful supply on the beaches. We had dispensation, with care, to collect logs from the beach and fill in the gaps. There were a couple of old metal carts, and we were able to load them up and wheel our fresher material to its destination. It was impressive to watch Carling, an Olympic sculler and full-on Amazonian, shoulder tree trunk-sized logs and effortlessly saunter off the beach and fill in the bigger gaps, putting the rest of us to shame. It was a collective effort though, and by lunchtime we had finished the markings.

When we went to set up for lunch, we got our next surprise. The lighthouse and wildlife trusts had organised the delivery of several pizzas for us, driven out by a small buggy. It had felt generous to allow us just to stay, but this? The guy who came out on the buggy to deliver them was none other than the ranger who had guided me as to where I needed to set off from the lower end of the spit the week before. There was a lot of happiness and plenty of smiles as we got stuck in. It sounds trivial to say it, but the pizza was still hot too.

Drew arrives to be greeted by Ian with pizza.

While we were eating, Drew – Team Arm and Leg – came into view. I was still feeling guilty for ratting out on him the day before, and when he got near enough, we went down to the yellow poles, taking half a pizza with us. When he landed his boat was as full of seawater as mine had been. Once we'd got his boat clear of the water, he stood eating his well-earned slices and I apologised. There was no rancour. It was the first proper conversation I got to have with him, and he was a lovely, garrulous guy. I resolved not to break any deal on paddling partnerships with him again.

That afternoon we carried on with the tasks we were offered. I spent some time with Leigh, Clare and Drew de-weeding the pond, using rakes to scoop out a barrowload and expose the rocks at the bottom. Clare got more stuck in, rolling up her trousers and wading in to remove handfuls of the stuff. As we finished, we were entertained by some of the smaller sea birds who took the opportunity to drink, swooping down and taking beakfuls of water with perfectly judged arcs over the pond. I tried to catch it on camera, but they managed to thwart my every effort.

Weeding the pond with Leigh and Claire from "Don't Tell Mom"

Later that afternoon we could see other crews roll in - the sailors. Two of the girls from Sockeye came ashore for a while but went back out that evening to sleep on their boat. I think in all there were three boats moored in the lee of the spit that night. It appeared with our lower profiles on the water we were able to sneak under the wind in a way the small sailboats were unable to manage. I have no idea if they rowed or tacked their way to Dungeness, but their day had certainly been more brutal than ours the day before. The media crew showed up, did a couple of interviews, and took a picture of our group. I met Rebecca, one of the field reporters, who asked a question or three about the day, the boat, and the Zen Dog poem, before catching the Zodiac back to the mainland. I recall Michelle braving a swim in the evening, but I was too much of a wimp to take a plunge.

There were opportunities through the day to chat with each other about approaches to the following morning, and tactics for the main crossing. The forecasts were all pointing to calm winds. We had the tide charts and the maps out, and the Oaracle were giving the best guidance to me as to how to proceed. The tidal variation was going to be the biggest in decades the next day, and we would have to factor in how the current shifted our direction. It was clear that within three hours of leaving our shelter we were going to be sat on a rapidly Westward shifting body of water.

There were also opportunities to properly meet these guys. Off the water, to a person they were easy-going, quiet, and amicable. Except possibly Drew, who was as garrulously and extravert as an American could get, in the best possible way. It was easy to warm to them all and a pleasure to have this downtime with them.

After dinner, more coffee, and more muffins than we could eat, we bedded down in the lighthouse for our last night before the crossing. Again, I found it hard to sleep, mainly because of the nervousness and anticipation of what the morning would bring, but also because we now had a rhythmical ensemble in residence, comprised of Ian on snores and Drew on breathtakingly regular farts. All this in stereo as Drew was on one side, Ian on the other. It wouldn't have changed my insomnia. Tomorrow promised all the ingredients of the most epic paddling day yet.

Field Report: A Silver Lining After a Rough Start

June 17, 2022 By Rebecca Ross, Field Reporter

On day two, I hopped on 'Ripsaw' the 15' RHIB and made my way to meet the small row teams stuck on Dungeness Spit—waiting for the foul weather to subside. I imagined the teams hunkered down against the wind, aimlessly shielding sand from tainting their food while sitting on a wet log. They've got to be cold and miserable out there.

Shortly after reaching shore, I spotted Clare and Leigh from Team Don't Tell Mom, smiles plastered on their faces. The two greeted me immediately before leisurely decorating their boat with an R2AK flag. Definitely not the scene I was imagining.

"How did it go out there?" I asked Leigh, her smile going strong.

"The crossing was rugged, it started out pretty well, but then the winds got worse. Three to four-foot waves mostly until they turned into five to six-foot waves. We took lots of waves over the bow, got soaked, and had to bail a lot. It was some of the toughest rowing I've done," she replied.

I turned around and met Team Let's Row Maybe?: Carling and Michelle. "So, what was it like?" I questioned.

Carling's description corroborated Leigh's, "We were good until it slowly started to get rough. And in the back of my mind, I knew I get seasick and was like, 'Oh no!' But I knew if I focused on the horizon, it would be okay. But then the swells started to get so big I couldn't see over the horizon, and I was like, WHAT DO I LOOK AT? THERE'S NO HORIZON!" Carling later explained that moments after turning the corner around Protection Island, she had lost her breakfast.

Needing more, I pried further, inquiring why they all looked so happy.

"Well, let us show you around," Michelle offered.

I followed the teams to Sequim Lighthouse and viewed their sleeping quarters inside an exhibit—dry, warm, and level—practically a four-star hotel compared to sleeping outside. Bob and Blaine, the lighthouse crew, had graciously welcomed the company of cold, miserable racers as they initially came to shore with open arms and an order of four large pizzas and enough muffins to feed an army. I'm starting to understand why this place is full of content racers.

Splitting off, I met up with Bob from Team Zen Dog and got his story. Cutting straight to the chase, Bob simply replied with a chuckle, "I was scared shitless."

"And how about now?" I asked.

Moments lapsed as I watched Bob leisurely reorganize his boat, stopping in between to tell me a story. Bob explained that people in a race often focus on the finish line—including in Race to Alaska. He further shared a moment that would be a "photographer's dream," describing part of the race where he witnessed a golden hour that had turned the river and the sides of the canyon gold. Deciding he no longer wanted to rush but instead appreciate the moment. "...because life is about building beautiful memories like this," Bob said as he looked toward the racers and lighthouse crew gathered on the plush lawn of the lighthouse, eating dinner while sharing laughs between bites. I get it now.

As the Race to Alaska continues, with undoubtedly loads of adverse weather and uncertainty—at that moment, with everyone enjoying their time on Dungeness Spit—it felt like there was a silver lining after such a crazy storm.

(Courtesy of Race to Alaska website)

Daily Update Stage 1, Day 2: Brunch fatigue, learning curves, and the citizens of Dungeness Spit

If your day was anything like ours, the second day of the R2AK 2022 started with a 5 am call with the Coast Guard just to make sure things hadn't gotten worse. They hadn't.

Talk to The Man, then peel back the eyelids with cup after cup after cup after cup after cup of as-strong-as-it-can-be/can-it-be-stronger coffee. Likely a bad idea, but if we could have poured coffee into our eyes we would have. No, we didn't try it. Really. Probably. R2AK. It's been a day...

Regardless of the coffee-stained pupils, when day dawned on Day Two of R2AK, our bleary-eyed snooze bar went from "Where are they and what do they think they are doing?" to "What are they doing in Victoria?" to "What are they doing on that beach?" to "How much brunch can they possibly have?" Depending on where they were, race teams' realities seemed vastly different.

In case your internet is oddly relegated to this specific part of our website, what you don't know until now is that after the epic wind and rescue fest of Day One, weather and waves split R2AK's class of 2022 into roughly three groups: the teams that made it to Victoria, the teams that went home, and the teams in the balance. On Monday, the first and successful that made it were treated to the warm embrace of Canada that included the stern talking to of the Canadian Coast Guard. To unjustly summarize the maple-leafed epaulets' words:

Don't be idiots.

It's a big coast and there aren't that many of us. There's more Coast Guard in the 40 miles of Stage One than the 700 of Stage Two. Make better choices.

*Wear a drysuit. Hypothermia is real and we don't search for bodies. (*sponsor plug* in case you're wondering: make it a Mustang drysuit; the driest drysuits in the world. Better yet: buy it at Fisheries Supply)*

The rest of the fleet? At time of writing, seven teams are still within a stone's throw of yesterday's starting line—safe and dry, and likely tiring of Port Townsend's brunch options. What was prudence on Day One is turning into the first-world problem of brunch fatigue as Day Two turns itself into Day Three's second-guessing: how is two days of not moving "Racing" to Alaska? Things are looking good even for those who have moved past Port Townsend's known breakfast options, especially for the 10-ish teams that made the Dungeness Spit their home for the last 36 hours; with more heading that direction to stage themselves for the cross border jump on R2AK's unprecedented Day Three.

For the 98% of everyone unfamiliar with the place, Dungeness Spit is a five-mile-long, wind-swept anomaly and the best/only refuge teams can get from a westerly wind and sea between Port Townsend and the "Done, thank god" breather of Victoria's inner harbor. There is a lighthouse with an actual light, a house for the lighthouse keeper, and at least today, a small and active colony of R2AK who all became at least temporary citizens in the Republic of Dungeness.

If brunch was the unifying truth of R2AK's Port Townsend-based teams, camaraderie was the throughline for the Citizens of Dungeness. After hitting the beach responsibly between the designated and yellow-painted posts that demarcated the landing area inside of the wildlife sanctuary, teams unfolded themselves into the fleeting and lighthouse-based community. In case the last sentence has you at "What the hell is a lighthouse-based community?" you're not alone. Until we saw it first-person, we'd have said the same thing.

Imagine a picket-fenced 100×300' patch of the softest and clearly manicured grass in the middle of a driftwood-infested middle of nowhere. It's like England established a croquet field in the tidal hinterlands of the Salish Sea. No, teams couldn't pitch tents on the immaculately mowed lawn (bird sanctuary, + England, etc) but they were of course invited to sleep in the museum. While the wind raged in the anchorage, beachable teams slept warm and dry, not to mention an all-access pass to the toolroom to fix the parts that shook loose in the washing machine that was Day One.

In the lee of the lighthouse, the scene on the spit looked a little like a Jetboil-themed beach party, and the stories that emerged confirmed all we had suspected and more about what happened in the first-est part of the race.

Yes, the tide rip was rough, but teams that hugged the beach were able to hard charge to the cold comfort of the US coast for the better part of their last three human-powered hours. To a team, the story of Stage One was, "It was ok, and then..." Even in the relative shelter of Dungeness Spit, human powering against the winds was a hatefest. "It was the hardest paddling I've ever done."

They all got there, but rowing into a stiff headwind for the last couple of hours was frustrating at best "I'd see the same piece of kelp for like four strokes." ...and that's to mumble through the epic seasickness. At least half of Team Let's Row Maybe was a technicolor yawn away from calling it quits. "I wanted to die." She rowed through chunk-blowing discomfort for hours. Hours. Hardcore and horrible rarely exist in so concentric of circles.

Upon arrival, the temporary residents of Dungeness revelled in the shelter and hospitality from members of the Dungeness Lighthouse Society who drove down on the low tide beach to deliver muffins and pizza (we can't make this stuff up.) In return, racers pitched in to rebuild a couple of walking trails. For the teams ashore, life was a wonderment of a dry sleep and pepperoni. For the not quite beachable, Dungeness offered the best/worst anchorage Stage One had to offer.

Yes, the weather was waning, but Tuesday night offered the bouncy, sleep-killing remnants of the weather system of the days before. For the non-beachable, the Dungeness anchorage offered a cold and bumpy comfort. "This is pretty miserable—one star!" was Team Dark Star's review. Even the prudent teens onboard Mustang Survival's Team Rite of Passage anchored at least twice because their anchor dragged and dragged again.

As nautical and civil twilight eek their way into the 0430, bleary-eyed, and Coast Guard sanctioned Strait crossing reality, citizens of greater Dungeness are headlamped and repacking dry bags to decamp and make the final push across. By the ordained go time for crossing, forecasts are calling for something between the decrescendo tail end and nothing. The saltwater and helicopter-rescued hellscape of the last 48 hours has fled the scene, the homestretch to Victoria has a rising barometer, falling winds, and a predicted >1' seas. This is as calm as the Juan de Fuca gets, and it's possibly your fault.

Yes, you.

Somewhere in your house is that light switch that you have no idea what it does. While we can't be certain, it's just possible that it's the on/off for R2AK wind. For the love of the deity/atheist figure of your choice, please leave it alone today. Rowboats gotta row.

At time of writing, there are eight hours and 40 flat calm miles between the furthest teams and Victoria's glory land. Light a candle, say a human-powered prayer they arrive in time, and for god's sake don't touch that light switch.

(Courtesy of Race to Alaska website)

Day Three: Dungeness to Victoria – 25 Miles

See you on the other side

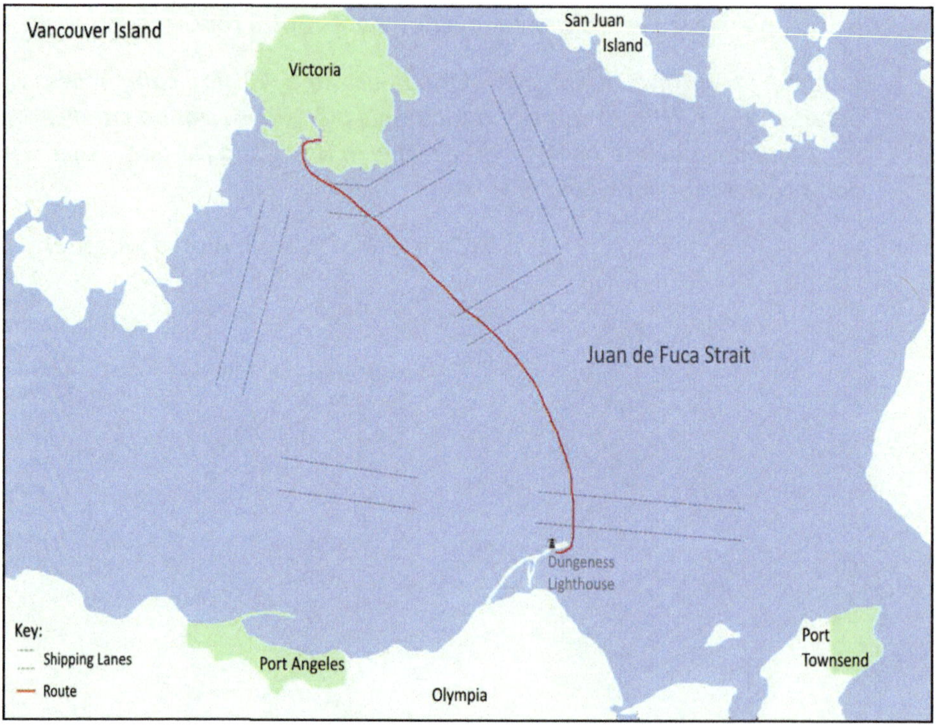

I was the first up that morning, and quietly began packing my sleeping gear at about four am. Drew was not long behind, and soon there were the sounds of sleeping mats being deflated and sleeping bags being stuffed in to their sleeves. I took time to chow down a breakfast bar, which required time as I'd brought with me what turned out to be the stodgiest bars going, demanding about half an hour to polish off. Boy, they were heavy on the stomach and hard work to chew. I shuttled between the lighthouse and the boat to load my gear, then donned my drysuit and waited at the beach. The sky was turning an ethereal blue as dawn took a hold of the day. The wind had abated. The day had all the hallmarks of being calm and clear. Looking back at the lighthouse down the paths we had revamped the day before was a beautiful sight. The lighthouse boys were awake and down on the beach to see us all off. Those guys had made our sojourn so special that it's hard to thank them enough for what they'd done.

Dawn before crossing Juan de Fuca.

Drew appeared, and I think it was in that moment he suggested that we paddle this leg together. Having let him down before, and in part because I knew I couldn't keep pace with Oaracle, there was never a question in my mind of saying "No". I knew from our conversations and from following the 2019 race that he'd been one of the crews to not make it to Victoria because of the weather in his previous attempt. It was impossible not to emotionally invest in him succeeding this time. We helped each other shift our boats onto the water and said our farewells to Blaine and Chip. It was properly daylight by the time we made the point.

I have no recollection of seeing the rowers on the Strait that day, and only the odd glimpse of a sailboat through the entire crossing. Today was about us kayakers, and at the outset, for the first hour, about the solos, me and Drew. Our first obstacle was a small race over shallower water, which was choppy without being challenging. Then came the first of the shipping lanes.

With Drew on Juan de Fuca from the Oaracle. Courtesy of Janice Mason

There were several shipping lanes between us and Victoria, clearly marked on the nautical charts, included in the race packets, and highlighted at the skippers meeting. Each one is about a mile wide, and we were looking out for the big guys, tankers, container ships, and the like from either direction. It was like playing a giant version of slow-motion Frogger. On this first lane one ship passed Eastwards before we were close enough for it to be an issue, and then the coast was clear. Less than quarter of an hour later we'd cleared it and were looking at the map for the next one.

I was following Oaracle's wisdom, reinforced by Drew, that the tidal changes to come were going to sweep us Westward from after seven that morning, so to counter it we needed to aim further East. In simple terms this meant aiming at the right-hand side of Juan de Fuca Island, which on the compass was near enough North. Juan de Fuca Island is about ten miles East of Victoria, so this was a leap of faith to me that we were not overcompensating for the impending current change.

We stopped occasionally for Drew to notionally ask me about where we were headed, but in reality, he was calling the shots, and I was readily agreeing to where he was targeting. Occasionally we stopped to eat, to drink, or to take a photograph or two. Ian and Janice were behind us for a while, then alongside… never too far away.

As the hours passed the target of Juan de Fuca Island did not change, but our bearing did. For almost the entire crossing, until we were only a couple of miles from the Vancouver Island shoreline, it was our target, and by the end I think we were almost paddling North-Eastwards towards it. The shipping lanes demanded higher effort levels, and during the last one I was convinced that there was a tanker speeding towards us, only to finally realise that it was at anchor and the tide was deceiving me.

Finally, what felt like about a mile from the coast, Drew called for a change of bearing to head North-West to Victoria. He and Oaracle were out-powering me, steaming ahead and then waiting as I caught up. It was still at least a further hour before we reached the beacon at the end of the harbour wall, but there was never any concern over making it there, nor about the weather conditions. We cruised into the harbour just before ten o'clock, and paddled in to the customs dock, all of half a mile from the finish.

In previous years Canadian Customs had allowed crews to register their arrivals at the finish in front of the Empress Hotel. This year, we were required to stop at the customs dock and phone in from there. It was a stop we couldn't miss. There was a rumour doing the rounds that one crew, Tri Baby Tri, a solo entry whose other incarnation was as a porn star, did fail to stop and register their arrival when landing at one of the islands, and found themselves unceremoniously removed from the country shortly thereafter. Every human-powered craft was there when we arrived, on their phones and waiting to speak to Customs. It took each of us over half an hour to get through to our respective customs officials, and in the case of Don't Tell Mom, double that as they lost their phone connection and consequently their place in the queue. I sat on the dock rather than wait in my boat, not trusting myself with my phone over water. Most of us had the experience of answering most of the customs questions before they twigged that we were in the R2AK. When they did, it was the same reaction: "Why didn't you say so?" Would it have made a difference to the speed of our processing? I guess not.

It felt like a full hour had passed by the time I had the green light to continue, and most of the others had already moved on. Drew, bless him, had waited for me so we could finish together. We paddled up to the dock at Victoria Causeway Marina and the finish of leg one just before eleven. We had polished off the second half of Stage One in half the time it had taken me to do the first leg, and its burden, which I felt like I'd been carrying for three years, slipped from my shoulders. After Drew had rung it, I was handed the bell to announce my arrival and its completion. I was qualified for the second leg, had avoided what I had worried would be the ignominy of elimination on the Proving Ground, and I was not done yet. It was definitely game on.

Victoria

There is certainly a great deal of anxiety at this moment.

We made our way around to the back of the dock, right by the harbour wall, and moored up. It was a glorious day now, and I clambered onto the pontoon in bright sunshine. All the sailing teams were moored up down the front, and the rowers and kayakers round the back. I think Lilian had made it by this time; her boat was in the corner by the foot ramp. That meant the full complement of human-powered solos was moving on to Stage Two.

I had booked a backpackers' hostel in town well in advance of the trip, and although Ian had offered me to stop at his place for another night, I knew he was stacked with his own preparatory tasks and didn't want to add to his list of things to worry about, so declined. I happily shed the drysuit which had been slow cooking me all morning and loaded what I needed into my Ikea bags. There were clothes to wash, kit to dry, and bits to wear for the next twenty-four hours. Although his race was complete, Drew was staying somewhere closer, and I think more upmarket than my lodgings, before he headed for home the following day. We agreed to meet up for lunch as soon as we'd gotten checked in.

I tramped through town to the Backpackers Hotel. The Ikea bags were good for short distances but harder work for the mile I had to cover to my hotel, especially with the weight of the wet gear inside. The hotel was everything it was cracked up to be, not in the most salubrious part of town, metal-grilled gates on the stairways, flimsy doors and thin walls, but cheap at twice the price and exactly what the doctor ordered. I hung out my kit and grabbed a quick shower. I pored over the maps as I adjusted the contents of the map case to bring the Victoria exit to the fore and skimmed the further reaches of the second leg. It was like opening Pandora's Box. I'll readily admit that a hefty weight of my focus had been on the first leg because of its immediacy, and it had carried some potentially treacherous challenges. Now it was done, and all of the monsters on Leg Two presented themselves simultaneously in my brain. Seymour Narrows and its whirlpools, Dixon Entrance, and above all looking at the maps, Cape Caution. I suddenly had no confidence that I could do this. How was I to tackle Cape Caution? I had a route, but with what tidal pattern should I consider setting out? I knew I would have to sit a mile or two from shore to avoid the boomers, the waves that suck the water off the rocks and smash straight into them, but how should I judge it? I knew I couldn't hold a candle to Oaracle and the power unit that is Janice Mason, and in all probability wasn't going to keep up with them. Daunting was an understatement. My confidence in myself, even after that morning's successful transit, hit rock bottom. With apprehension back on the agenda I headed back into town to find Drew.

There were less than twenty four hours until the start of the race proper, and there were tasks I needed to complete before the bell rang to send us on our way. First though, we needed to savour what we'd done. The pair of us sat down in a nearby restaurant, demolished a good-sized lunch, and celebrated the last two days. It must have felt equally, if not more, satisfying for Drew to have completed what he'd set out to do in 2019. I wish he'd been carrying on for the next leg because he was a pleasure to paddle with, and he was generous in his help and support in the crossing and again in Victoria.

I picked up the missing items on my list. My watch was hanging on to my wrist by a gaffer-taped thread, and I found an almost like-for-like replacement. I found a water bottle for the deck which I could put electrolytes in: I didn't dare risk clogging up the filters on the dromedaries for fear of not having access to purified drinking water.

The rest of that afternoon passed in a flash, and before we had time to blink it was five o'clock and time for the additional skippers briefing. Had things gone to plan and the weather not intervened, this would have been with all the sailing crews the previous day. As it was, the crews that had made landfall in Victoria that day, including many of the Angus Row Cruisers, assembled by the fountain to hear from Daniel. The gist of the briefing was as per the coastguard briefing in the film: be careful. The coastguard only searches for live people. They do not search for bodies. It was sobering to hear again about the scarcity of a safety net from Campbell River onwards.

Lilian was there, and I voiced my concerns about my capabilities for the coming days and suggested that maybe we team up for safety in numbers. Her response was a flat-out "No". I could relate to the reasoning that she saw it as a solo race, and solo meant solo, not rowing or paddling with any other person. I had no complaint about this, but it had been worth a shot to ask. Of all the teams, she was the one who was most likely to have been similar paced. I didn't concern myself with asking anyone else.

That evening we found ourselves with the Don't Tell Mom ladies and Lilian in a Chinese restaurant in town. Lilian's other half, Dave, was also in town. After dinner, despite feeling shattered, I headed to the basement of the hotel with my washing to complete the last of my chores. Dave appeared for the same purpose, and we chatted idly for a while. As the clock ticked round to eleven, and the clocks on the dryer counted down to zero, I tried to keep my eyes open, and it was all I could do to not nod off in the laundry room. Adrenaline and nerves weren't going to prevent a good night's sleep this time.

Dockside in Victoria. Minnie is just to the left of the gangway

Thursday. Race Day. I was awake early, and I could swear I could hear Dave and Lilian talking through the walls. It didn't take me long to grab a shower and pack up my gear. It took a while longer though, to lug the bags down to the dock. Minnie was up on the deck, and I re-floated her to load her up. Everything in the Ikea bags was packed in drybags of all shapes and sizes, and I now knew that Helen had ninja'd the lot of them with messages of support from family and friends. You could rely on Helen to come up with a good old pick-me-up motivational brainwave when you needed it. I resolved not to read them all in one hit, but to savour them as the trip unfolded. It was the first time I'd tried to fill her hatches from a dock rather than on a beach, and the combination of the bounce of the boat on the water and the awkward angles I was having to lean over at made it nigh on impossible to pack. The ten-minute process I had practiced on Patrick's drive for packing was taking a lot longer, and I started to panic about fitting everything in. In the end, I emptied Minnie again, pivoted her up onto the dock, loaded the far reaches of the hatches, and re-floated her.

Jennifer from team Fashionably Late collared me and presented me with a small bottle and a coaster. The coaster had instructions for how to make a cocktail using the contents of the bottle, and a barcode linking to a playlist of music to listen to while drinking it, a really classy gesture. I did feel that the bottle of Zen Dog beer I had stashed in the front of Minnie which I had expressly to hand to Jake or Daniel at the finish would trump it. Yet I only had the one bottle, and I felt a little guilty at not being able to reciprocate. Mercifully there was enough space in the day hatch for the bottle and coaster to fit. Thank you, Fashionably Late!

There now wasn't a great deal to do before the race start at midday. Everyone else was busy, so I went off to eat what I could, and try and keep a lid on the nerves. I remember little of that morning beyond sitting and drinking coffee in a café not far from the start. I had not been this nervous before a race for a long, long time. There was nothing more I could do in preparation.

By half past eleven I had my drysuit on and had gone to the top of the steps to wait for the start. I was the only racer there. I felt like a gooseberry around the few sensibly clad pedestrians walking past. It was as though nothing were about to happen, just a normal day at the top of those steps. It didn't help that it was a warm day, and I was beginning to boil in my drysuit bag.

As twelve approached teams began to gather. The usual “good luck” banter, handshakes, and hugs were exchanged. Daniel stood up, and made a rousing send-off speech, as only Daniel can. The countdown was chorused by all of us from ten. The time had come. The Race to Alaska was “Go”.

16 June -The Race to Alaska

Day One : Victoria to Prevost Island – 38 Miles

We are go, repeat, go!

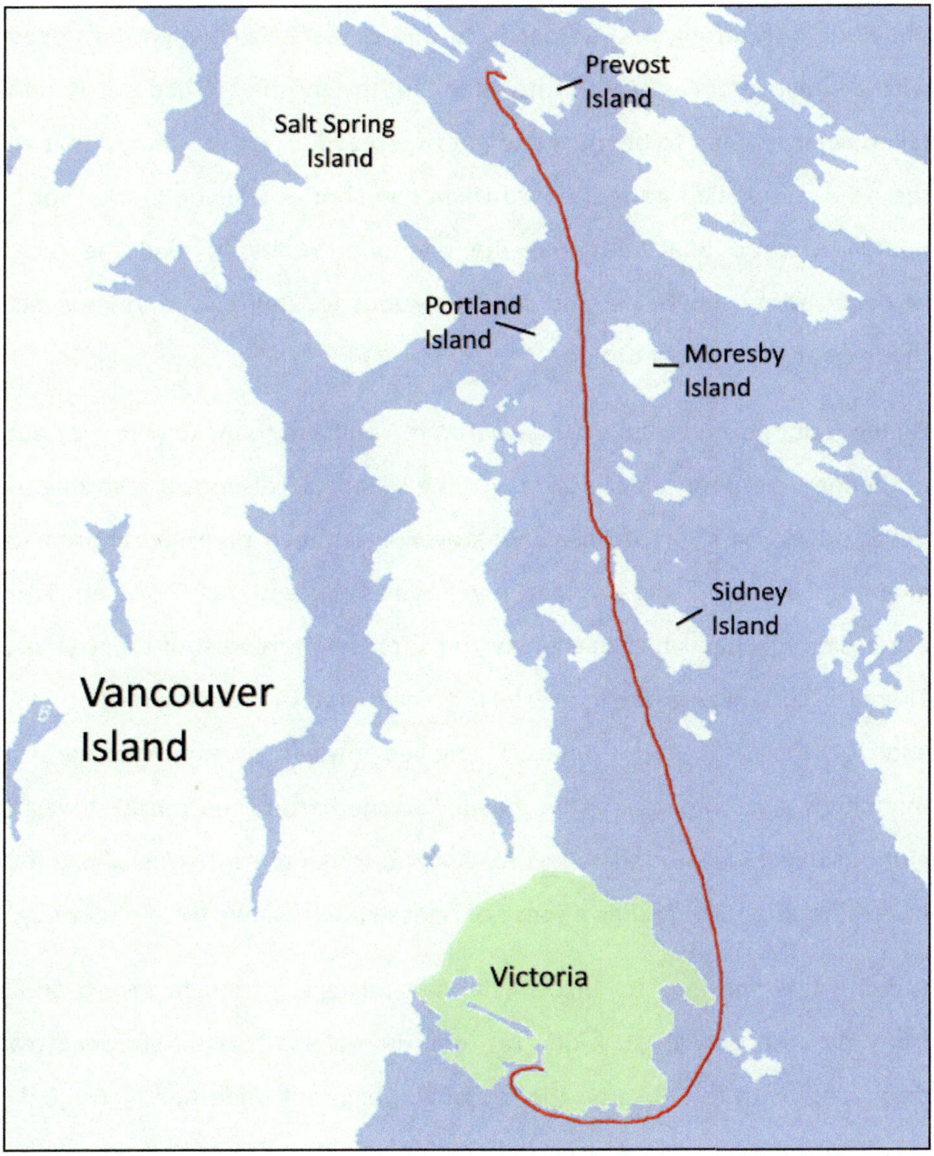

Leg Two begins with a Le Mans start from the top of the docks to your boat before heading out into the harbour. I had no intention of running, and I had no desire to take part in the melee and scramble of crews sprinting to their boats. Fifty metres of sprinting would buy me nothing. I lingered at the back of the trampling herd, reaching Minnie as many of the crews were casting off. It's a faff getting into a boat from a dock, especially when it's ridged with a small retaining wall on its edge, and by the time I had got in and taken what seemed to be an age to get my spraydeck on, it seemed that all the other crews had gone. I noted Lilian had shot out of the blocks. For a human-powered boat, this was the one opportunity to lead the race, however brief it might be, and take the kudos for doing so, and I suspect that's what she'd set out to do.

Sailing is not permitted in Victoria Harbour. You have to make your way out of the inner harbour under power. For the sailboats, this meant resorting to pedal drives, oars, or paddles... whatever alternative they had chosen to engines. For me it meant that my paddles were a far more efficient propulsion mechanism than their systems for the narrowest of timeframes. There is a certain pleasure in overtaking bigger craft in the same race as you, and for the next three miles I enjoyed myself passing catamarans, monohulls, and trimarans as we headed to the harbour entrance. It was a glorious day. I was not searching for anyone to paddle with, just doing my own thing, and I was feeling a sense of release now that we were underway.

It didn't take me long to uncover my first mistake. I tried to take a drink from my hose only to suck on air. I quickly realised that I'd strapped my dromedary with the hose on the top of the bag, not underneath. The only way I could get a drink was to press hard down with my legs to pressure the water up through the hose. This wasn't going to be a satisfactory workaround for long. Thankfully it was calm enough that I was able to stop, unclip the bag, flip it over and re-seal my deck.

I cleared the harbour wall and turned Eastwards. It didn't take me too long to reel in Lilian. I think I caught her at her hour break, as she took time to stand up and stretch. We chatted for a couple of minutes before I pulled on ahead. I could see Oaracle ahead, but today I was going to do my own thing, and I was content, if not a little hot in my drysuit.

Catching up with Lilian, who was taking a break, outside Victoria.

Maps play funny games with your mind. When I prepared mine for the race, I printed what I considered to be the more important sections on a larger scale, and the stretch from Victoria was one of them. Riding the tide Eastwards definitely helped, but the sheer speed I was clearing each bay on the map was making the afternoon feel effortless. As I rounded Gonzales

Point by Victoria Golf Club and headed into the Gulf Islands, I saw Oaracle peel off into Oak Bay to make a pit stop. I was now completely alone; there was no sign of any of the other racers, and it felt like there were very few other boats nearby. After all of the fear and worry about being on my tod, I was feeling completely in my element and at home on my lonesome.

I'd anticipated the illusion of the slowing of time paddling on the sea compared to my usual forays on the canal, which was just as well. I spotted a large buoy a way ahead, and it took over an hour to reel it in and overtake it. At one point I could see on the maps that I was entering a section of tidal race. In all the sessions I'd done in Anglesey, there'd been the "rule" that paddlers of my ability were not to go into them unsupervised. I felt like a naughty schoolkid tittering and paddling into the ripples, accelerating through the narrower channels, feeling like toothpaste squeezed out of a giant tube.

You could see this blighter from miles (and hours) away. Beyond Oak Bay. Day One.

I had several campsites earmarked for that evening, dependant on how good a time I was able to make through the afternoon. By six o'clock I'd settled on Prevost Island over Portland Island, the same location Matt Pruis had used back in 2018. It was still at least an hour away, and there was plenty of daylight left. Standing on Matt's shoulders was a huge bonus. Not only was I virtually guaranteed a decent pitch, but I could gauge my schedule against his. Having not had a clue what my daily mileage might be before the race, I now had a benchmark of what each day could possibly look like.

By the time I rolled by the beginnings of Prevost Island the fatigue from the day's exertions was kicking in. The island had four bays, all facing out to the North-West. I plumped for the third one, and as I passed the headland to turn into it, I saw a stag standing on the bank. It was my first wildlife of the second leg, and totally not the sort of creature I'd expected to encounter there.

The bay I'd picked was lined with trees down both sides, ending in a large grassy meadow, with a solitary tree smack bang centre near the water's edge. I paddled past the cruisers and yachts moored nearer the entrance and beached to the left of centre and the left of tree. There followed the chaos of an inexperienced kayak tourer making his first solo landfall. I disembarked, cleared a bunch of gear into an Ikea bag, and carried it some way up into the grass away from the tideline. I was fearful of high tide floating my gear away. I shifted the boat up into the grass, before realising there would be nothing to tie it up to. I looked left into the trees, then right, settling on a pitch by the water that looked like it would take my hammock. I then shifted Minnie back to the tree and tied her up, reasoning that even if she re-floated, she'd not go anywhere. I then relayed the bags, sloshing through the swampy, bug-ridden grass several times, to the trees. With hindsight, it would have been so much more sensible to just moor up by the trees, but I was green, inexperienced, and this was part of the learning curve.

I set my stove boiling water and set up my hammock. I was content, but the fatigue – particularly from the last hour – was kicking in. My wilderness camping inexperience wasn't over. It was time to think about the bears. In the lead-up to R2AK, the question I was asked more than any other was "What about the bears?" It was inevitably a concern. I'd done my research and knew that I could use bear barrels or hoist my food into a tree, out of reach. I had plumped for the latter plan as barrels would take up too much space in the boat. I was glad there was nobody there to witness the comedy of what followed. There was only one tree that really fit the bill, leaning over at thirty degrees with a branch sticking up that would serve as a pulley point. I then spent the next half-hour trying to get my line over the bloody nook. It was embarrassing, but it wouldn't go, until finally I had the presence of mind to attach a drybag to the end of the line and throw that over. I then hooked all twenty-plus kilos to the end of the rope and tried to hoist it. The friction of the rope in the nook, combined with my tired arms and the finickitiness of tying the other damn end to another tree restricted my efforts. It took a further quarter of an hour to get it all of eight feet in the air. If there had been any bears nearby, and I'm fairly certain Prevost was bear-free that night, my suspended provisions would have been easy pickings. I put on some dry thermals, set my alarm for five, and crawled into my sleeping bag and hammock. Day One and thirty eight wholly satisfactory miles were done, and so was I. I went to sleep, oblivious to the presence less than a couple of hundred metres away of two other crews, Don't Tell Mom and Let's Row Maybe? tucked up in their sleeping bags in the next bay.

Day Two : Prevost to Protection Island, Nanaimo – 37 miles

L.O.S. All Systems go.

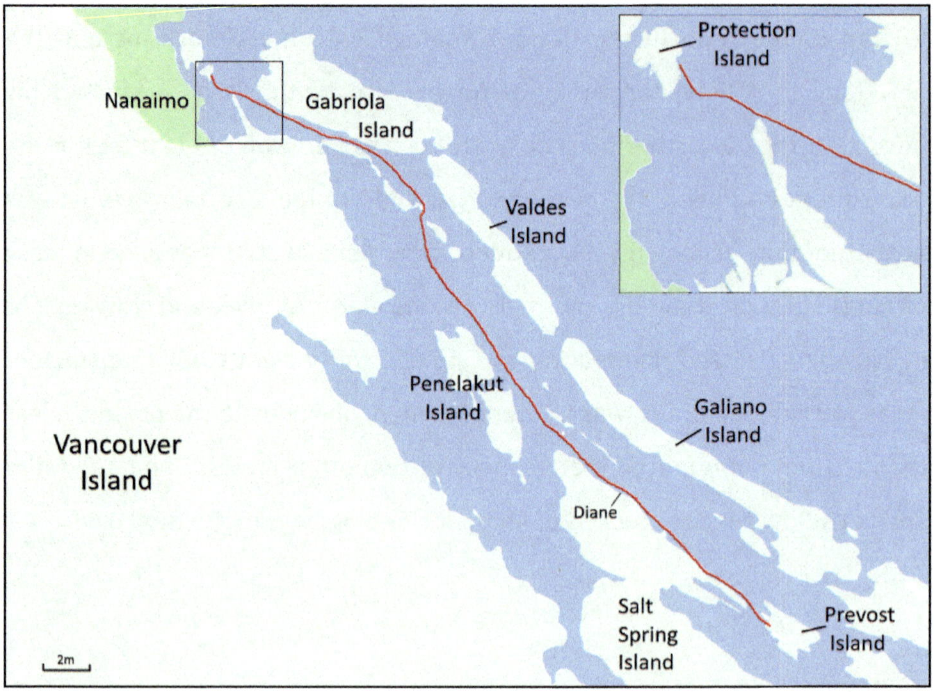

I woke pre-dawn and swung out of the hammock in to the darkness under the tree canopy. First job was coffee. The food bundles bumped down to earth, and I retrieved the stove and my AeroPress, which had its own dedicated bag. Ground filter coffee was my luxury item, and again Cousin Helen had come up trumps with a camping percolator. Over the next hour I struck camp and had my breakfast. It took the full hour to eat the breakfast bar because, while it had all the calories I wanted, it was so bloody stodgy. In between bites I reluctantly put my damp clothes from the day before back on. They were shiveringly cold for a few seconds before absorbing my body heat and becoming tolerable. I trudged back and forth through the reeds, the weed, and the swarms of insects to Minnie and loaded up. It was the beginnings of a clear day, but there was a North Westerly wind to contend with.

There was definitely fatigue in my shoulders and back as I crossed over to Saltspring Island, and the ten miles of it I had left to pass. I was in Trincomali Channel now, sheltered from the Strait of Georgia by Galiano Island, beyond which lay Vancouver. The tide was definitely against me, and that wind was blowing strongly against me too. I reminded myself of the first day. This wasn't so bad.

As I paddled up Saltspring, a Zodiac appeared with the media crew on board, including Rebecca. "You're crushing it!" she yelled over the noise of the engine. I wasn't quite sure what to say. I was doing my own thing, and there was nobody about but our two boats. I hope I was civilised enough to exchange some pleasantries; it was still before eight and I was very much in "still waking up" mode, or at least my muscles were. They bombed off, leaving me in a pleasant solitude, but it had been lovely to be on the receiving end of those positive vibes.

Shortly after, I spotted an open-sided hut that would have made an ideal stopping point, wistfully thinking about the hassle of hauling those bags into the tree. There'd always be plenty of better alternatives. Be happy with your lot. Best to park those thoughts and move on.

At about 10:30, I could see a jetty ahead. My maps weren't always the most helpful with names because I'd plumped for nautical charts over land ones, but this appears to have been Fernwood Point. At a distance I could see the silhouettes of a couple of people at the top of the ramp, and as I drew closer, one of them started frantically waving at me. I pulled in as she shouted:

"Zen Dog! Zen Dog! I've got a cup of coffee and a piece of banana bread for you!"

I know all about R2AK tracker junkies. I am one, and have been for every race there's been, but this was the first time I'd really been on the receiving end of a local tracker junkie, and it was a sublimely uplifting moment. I swung into the side of the jetty out of the direct flow of the current and grabbed hold of the yellow step rail. Cue one Diane Gutiw, who had been following the race, saw I was passing, had grabbed the coffee and cake, and come down on spec to see me. It's hard not to be taken aback by her enthusiasm and generosity; I was flattered, slightly humbled, and grateful all at once.

Tracker Junkies are the best! Courtesy of Diane Gutiw

As I hung on to the jetty, she filled me in. I was leading the human powered crews! It explained why Rebecca had been yelling "You're crushing it" earlier, but this was bonkers. I'd seen what Ian and his JMPU could do, leaving me for dead on day one. As for the two two-woman row crews… I looked at the water in front of me, rushing past back in the direction I'd come from. I'd got something tactically wrong if this was the case. Maybe I was starting too early, as it was the only reason I had any advantage, getting up two hours before the others, and paddling more against the tide? No, this felt less than sensible to me, but at the same time, that little competitive imp in my brain was bouncing off the insides of my skull. I was leading something! I drank my coffee, and we talked about the race. Diane was the spirit lifter that morning, and I reluctantly headed on feeling very content.

At midday, as Saltspring finally petered out on my left, I crossed over to Jackscrew Island, found a small beach, and pulled in for lunch. I decided that I'd cook something warm, as I was struggling to eat my bars, and hot food seemed like a sensible plan. As the water stewed my pasta, I ate Diane's banana cake and called Helen to fill her in on the last twenty four hours. Before I could start, she told me my official tracker was not working. Dammit! It seemed like I'd have to do a reset every time I set foot in the boat. While we were yakking, I powered it off and on again. Presto! A signal.

Helen confirmed what Diane had told me; I was leading. Leigh and Clare weren't far behind, and while we talked, they passed on the far side of Jackscrew. I never saw them, given the angle of my little bay. She also told me how they'd camped a raccoon paw's distance from me on Prevost. While we talked, I ate my pasta, clambered back in, and paddled on.

Jackscrew lunch spot.

The afternoon passed in a series of islands: Mowgli, Norway, Penelakut, Rid, and Thetis, as I headed further up Trincomali. I spent a large portion of the afternoon bearing down on a tanker moored in the middle of the channel, which seemed to get no bigger or closer as time went by. I was hailed from behind, to find that Let's Row Maybe? had caught me up, and we took pictures of each other taking pictures of each other as they effortlessly cruised on by.

As I approached De Courcy Island I remembered that my notes from Miller, the Inside Passage bible, had suggested I avoid Dodds Narrows as it is the main shipping channel. I beached briefly to change maps, and for a while enjoyed the pleasure of being catapulted on the incoming tide through False Narrows into Northumberland Channel, just short of Nanaimo. I was tiring now, and it was closing in on six o'clock as I started to cross the ferry lines that ran into Nanaimo. As Gabriola ended, there was a decision to make about where to camp, and I favoured stopping at the campground on Protection Island, another Protection Island after day one, on the far side from Gabriola. It was a random choice for me, to pick this over the last camping points on Gabriola, but I'd spent my time marking the sites on my map so Protection it would be.

I'm fairly certain I saw Daniel in a Zodiac on that final crossing, but neither of us stopped. The fatigue of the day had well and truly kicked in, and the current started to pull me towards Vancouver Island, left of where I wanted to go. As I drew closer, I began to curse myself. The campsite was not visibly obvious on the Island and some prize berk, namely me, had marked its location in the centre of the island. Protection was close to a mile over, so I was facing up to another two miles around to find it. I picked out the one tree free spot on the nearside and headed for it.

There was a group of kids having a barbecue down by the shoreline as I reached it. I called out to them "where's the campsite?" If there was a reply, it's lost in my memory to what happened next. A voice to my left yelled "Robert!" I looked round to see a woman running down the shore, waving her arms and trying to get my attention.

"Zen Dog! Do you want to stop at my place?"

Enter stage left, Liz. By now, I'd become enough of a dirtbag to not turn down an offer like this. Hell, yes, and thank you! She directed me all of a hundred metres down the shore to the beach in front of where she lived. This night, there would be a witness to how chaotic my unpacking would be. Between us, we unloaded, got the boat out of the water and above the tide line. Bags went into the basement of her house, and my drysuit came off as I apologised for the smell after two days of boil in the bag paddling and wild camping.

Before we went any further, I got a selfie of the pair of us and posted it. This was the most special moment of the race to me. It took all of a minute for Helen to message me to tell me that she was glad I was sorted for the night. We stepped up into Liz's living room, while Liz explained to me how she'd watched me cross and realised how tired I was. She filled me in on where the others were. On her balcony was a telescope, and it was trained on Gabriola, on Let's Row Maybe's boat, moored up where they'd camped. Don't Tell Mom were close by. Ruf Duck were in Nanaimo Marina. Rite of Passage were passing through. I called Ian and Janice at that point, as Liz offered them camping too, but they'd already beached nearby for the night. The epitome of the die-hard tracker junkie, Liz was avidly following the race as it unfolded, and knew where we all were.

My most talked about encounter of the trip. With Liz on Protection Island

I had a warm shower. Bliss. She fed me chilli, put my smelly clothes in her washing machine, and we sat down with my maps that evening and discussed possible campsites for the next few days on the way up to Seymour Narrows. Liz was a kayaker and had paddled all of the coast I was about to tackle. We talked about blisters. My hands were beginning to feel the effects of the salt water, and the callouses I'd worked up in training over the previous months were beginning to dissolve in this more hostile saline environment. More importantly to me, we talked about Liz. It turned out her work, her passion, had connections close to home. Her research connected her to the London Tring Museum, not a stone's throw from my folks outside London. I'm still hoping that she will come visit, so we can return the hospitality of this wonderful evening. I think it was close to ten o'clock when the fatigue started to get the better of me, and I crashed out, not in my hammock, but in a bed. A luxurious end to a happy day.

"So, somewhere along this beach is where Zen Dog was last tracked to, and we are pre…tty sure that he has selected the, uh, ninja mode on his Spot tracker, and he is up there by Team Oaracle. But it was here that apparently someone came off the beach when he pulled in and said 'what are you doing? Come inside. You need a warm bed.' So I think his night was spent kind of cosy. So we are a little surprised he left. Thought he might just be aiming to stick around a bit longer."

(Daniel Evans, transcript of his update from the Protection Island Shoreline just opposite Liz's place, sometime after breakfast.)

We were up early, probably about 5:30. Liz carried on where she'd left off. I had granola with powdered milk for breakfast. Twice. I cannot stand powdered milk, but this was delicious, and went down so much more easily than my breakfast bars. During the course of conversation, we'd talked about how my deck leaked, and she produced a Seals Extreme Touring deck, something I'd been hankering after before the race, and some braces to hold them. She added some drip guards to my paddle shafts to stop the water running on to my hands. There are some rare, very special people in life, and Liz is one of those. Thank you, Liz.

We loaded the boat, and because it was raining, I added my poncho over my drysuit. Fortunately, fashion statements go unnoticed on the water, even if a picture or two made the race feeds later that day. I transferred my dromedary to the back deck. It was a nuisance under my legs for getting out and in, and it was just more convenient to have it to hand behind me. With my food arranged for the day in front of me, I set off.

The R2AK fashion statement. Not. Definitely practical though. Courtesy Liz Hammond-Kaarremaa.

Georgia Strait today promised few landmarks. The Gulf Islands ended at Nanaimo, and now I faced the best part of a day paddling with coastline only to my left. The usual aches took an hour to dull as my muscles woke up. After about an hour, I could see a rowing boat what felt like a mile further out to sea, parallel with me. I could make out it was Don't Tell Mom. For a while they just seemed to easily move past, and then they were lost behind the swells.

I passed Dolphin Beach and headed to Mistaken Island with a plan to stop there for lunch. However, I didn't spot a suitable cove to pitch up in, so I carried on down the coast. The next five miles were luxurious paddling. The wind was behind me today, and the shoulder rotations felt easy as I paddled down to French Creek. I knew there was a restaurant there, and my thought was to have a plate of chips and a burger. When I arrived, I baulked at paddling into the marina, which with hindsight I should have done, opting instead for the beach behind the harbour wall. Having lugged the boat clear, I repeated the previous day's lunchtime routine. Boil water. Hydrate food. Speak to Helen. Reset tracker. That tracker was a damned nuisance. I was giving it the good old "Microsoft Way" treatment at every opportunity, but it was a GPS zombie, and just kept going back to sleep. By the time Janice called to say they were in the restaurant, it was too late. I'd eaten and was about to set off again. It was rough, and the launch was tricky with the waves. It took some time to seal the deck without swimming, and I was off again.

> *"Um... so we found Zen Dog... French Creek... Came out to talk to him now. He's that little speck in front of the motor boat about to go over behind him. Um, that's Bob, Zen Dog. Zen Dog's zen state: Zen does not want to be found. So, we will continue the hunt for Zen Dog another day, but there he is. He's underway and moving North."*
>
> (Daniel Evans, from the harbour wall overlooking the beach, just after lunch.)

There were no islands at all that afternoon, save the two mountainous ones on the horizon I was headed for. I could see the south-eastern end of Denman Island, and to its right was Hornby Island. My immediate target was the marina at the tip of Hornby, not least because there was a rumour that a previous R2AK sailor was seeking out paddlers with some goodies to eat. My route took me over two miles offshore. The tailwind was strong now, and I was riding waves towards the islands. I was having to regularly correct as they were manipulating me off my tracking line on my Garmin, and I was working hard to maintain a course that bisected Denman and Hornby, checking frequently over my shoulder for traffic and rogue waves. I was comfortable, although I was still leaking water into the cockpit. Sadly, Liz's replacement deck was only marginally better than mine.

The VHF sprang into life mid-afternoon. It was the Coastguard, and they were responding to a report of a two-man white kayak, apparently in trouble as the paddler in the front had appeared to have lost their paddle. There was only one boat that I could think of that fit that bill, and its occupants had been eating chips and goodness knows what else in the restaurant behind me that lunchtime.

I was in a quandary. You're supposed to offer assistance to any vessel needing help. Here was a report of a scenario demanding exactly that, and I *knew* the people in question. I also had a spare paddle on the back of my boat. To counter that, Minnie's cockpit was again sloshing water around my legs, and I was a good two miles myself from shore. Not only that, but I had no idea where Oaracle were. I tried to radio back to the Coastguard, but I was out of broadcasting range and got no reply. At that point, I pulled a one hundred and eighty degree turn and scanned the horizon, looking for a white boat amongst the white caps bearing down on me. I couldn't see them and eventually, reluctantly, resumed my bearing towards Denman and Hornby. That I couldn't or didn't really do anything to help Oaracle was to gnaw away at me for the rest of the day. It was easy to make all sorts of excuses for not making more of an effort to seek them out, but the cold, hard bottom line was that I bottled going to help. I wasn't being the person I wanted to be in doing that, and it made me feel grubby.

By half past six I'd made the marina at Ford Cove, the foot of Hornby Island. I paddled into the shelter of the harbour between the moored-up boats, getting a few strange looks on the way. When I got close to the shore, I dug out the boat pump and emptied the cockpit of the gallons of water washing around my legs. There was now a decision to make. Should I stay here? I decided to get a mile or two further, in part because the tide was now in my favour, more because I was feeling quite fresh despite a full day's yomp, but mostly because Denman had a family connection. Distant cousins, several times removed, lived there. There might be an off chance they knew I was passing, even though race rules prevented me contacting them.

I crossed back over to Denman and found Fillongley campsite. I'd made no errors marking this one. There were campers on the beach, and I talked a couple of lads into helping get Minnie over the tide ridge. I set up my hammock on the beach and was cooking up dinner as Ian and Janice arrived. The worry I'd had all afternoon disappeared as Janice casually dismissed the whole incident. They'd had a visit from the coastguard to check on them, as there must have been a report from a well-meaning walker on the shore who hadn't seen a paddle in her hands. She was probably eating or checking the map. For them it was a non-issue, but for me? My reaction to that situation is still something that bothers me now.

Before crashing out for the night, I checked my phone. There was a call from a United States number that I didn't recognise, and I called it back. It was Lilian. She was further back, somewhere beyond French Creek, but way short of where I was. She asked if the offer to buddy up was still open. This was somewhat unexpected after the emphatic rejection of the idea earlier on. I was a little ambivalent about it; I'd got used to the solitary hours on the water. There was a lot still to come though. Seymour Narrows was nearly on top of me, and there was Cape Caution not far beyond. I agreed on the proviso that she caught me up at Campbell River the following evening. This was a wholly ungenerous offer on my part, but I was not going to sacrifice half a day waiting for her to catch up.

Day Four : Denman to Campbell River – 45 miles

I woke up at about five. As I went to open my mouth, I could feel that my lips were glued together. The sun and windburn over the previous week had gradually reduced them to a sticky, puslike mess, despite me applying lip sunblock and lip balm every half an hour. I went through the unpleasantness of parting my lips and feeling the scabbing peel away. It added to the aches, along with chafing from the backrest to my lower back, and from my drysuit to my right armpit, and of course the blisters and cuts on my hands. I was catching my fingers on the combing inside the hatches, and on small rocks on the shore. The callouses I had developed in training were continuing to dissolve in the salt water, as were the tips of my fingers. The ends had gone, leaving frayed bits near the tips, which came off easily. This was all part and parcel of the race. I knew that day, as with every day, I would set off, and after an hour the aches would subside as I warmed up. The blisters would just settle and heal, and I'd be fine. It would just be an hour of embuggerance before I got there. For now, I felt like I'd aged thirty years as I rotated out of the hammock and fiddled with my shoes to get upright and break camp.

Denman Island with Ian and Janice, just before setting out on Day Four

My distant family never materialised, but it meant no question about me receiving support, organised or not. I was ready for the water marginally ahead of Oaracle, and out in my boat as they finished loading up. It was a magnificent morning, the sun coming up on the far side of Georgia Strait, and the water was flat calm.

Georgia Strait, early on Day Four. If only conditions were always like this.

I recall I paddled ahead of them for a long time that morning, aiming for the headland below Comox airport. I knew Janice needed to stop and replace a spraydeck around there. It was a repeat of the night before in terms of landscape: the headland was there from the get-go, and it did not get closer for what seemed like an eternity. As we finally got there near midday, we spotted the media boat. Ian and Janice went and did their publicity thing, and I headed for the beach. Cooked lunches were now a fixture in my plans, and the beach looked good.

I cooked and ate, watching the walkers going past with their dogs, tracking the odd plane taking off overhead. When the coast was finally clear, it was time for a call of nature. I found a log suitable to perch on, and mid…er…flow, the media crew in the boat started hailing me. I hoped to goodness they didn't have a camera trained on me. It would not have made good publicity.

A bit lighter, refreshed, and reloaded, I paddled out to speak to them. Rebecca was there with Lynette, who I'd not really met yet. They filled me in on Campbell River. There was a ferry pier, and marinas behind, and I think I was supposed to aim for the third marina in line. We then did a short question and answer piece for the camera in exchange for more food, and I was off again.

It was roasting hot, and I was feeling the post prandial malaise from stopping, eating, and restarting. The drysuit was doing my head in, so it was not long before I was back on the shore, and the top was off for the first time all trip, tucked into the cockpit under the deck. This wasn't the safest arrangement, nor the most comfortable, so an hour later it was off altogether and rammed down between my feet. There was still no real space in the hatches for additional gear.

That afternoon was a grind, especially after yesterday had felt comparatively settled. I was paying for the long lunch break, and Ian and Janice were nowhere to be seen, presumably a long way ahead. It didn't help that my backside was freezing, and I couldn't figure out why. The coast was dead straight, and at one point my maps had a gap, meaning I didn't quite know the distance I had to cover. I'm sure that Janice had told me it was twenty miles. I think it was nearer thirty. Furthermore, I think the tide was not helping me. Passing Oyster River took forever, and when I finally got close to Cape Mudge it was against me for sure. Now there were logs, lots and lots of driftwood, congregating on the eddy lines I was staying inside of. There were patches where I was negotiating mini rapids plagued with logs, paddling up levels as the water spilled over as the tide pushed against me. It became easier to hug the shore and go through the mazes they formed than be further out in the current.

By the time I reached the jetty it was getting dark. I'd not paddled this late in the race, and I was the most tired I'd been yet. I counted past the marinas, one, two, and pulled in to the third one. I found a place to moor up, but it didn't feel right. I stepped out to find help and bumped into another crew who turned out to be a friend of a cousin and had been racing until they'd hit a log in Johnstone Strait, up ahead, and been forced to retire and turn back. Definitely a small world. I called Janice, who told me that they were in the first marina, along with the media guys, with access to showers. Reluctantly, as it was a mile, and a mile in the wrong direction at that, I retraced my steps and at around 8:30 moored up with them. It was a warm night. I borrowed the key for a shower and set up my hammock as a bivi on the dock. It looked a pitiful sight as a bivi, sagging badly in the middle and not really tied down well at all. Janice, bless her, took pity on me, and made me a hot chocolate. I was shattered, and in no mood to cook. In fact, I'd intended for some time, even before the race, that tonight I'd pay a homage to the legend who is Roger Mann.

Roger has nailed his place down in R2AK folklore. In 2016, he'd arrived in Campbell River in his boat, Happy Feet, hundreds if not thousands of calories short of his daily requirement of around six thousand. He'd shot past the waiting media crew, having spied the big yellow "M" not far from the marina, and ordered and eaten four Big Mac's, memorably commenting in the R2AK film, "I wish I'd got five". I had a yearning for a McDonald's, and I eschewed setting up my JetBoil in favour of a walk into town to pay my own homage to Mr Mann.

McDonalds was closed, and I was crestfallen. In desperation – I really did not want to cook – I bought a couple of bottles of coke and some crisps and sat on a bench in the park and tried to eat. Tired and aching, I slouched back to my bivi and hunkered down for the night. Sleeping on the ground wasn't nearly as comfortable as being suspended between two trees. Sleep was fitful, but eventually I was out for the night.

Day Five : Campbell River to Elk Bay – 25 miles

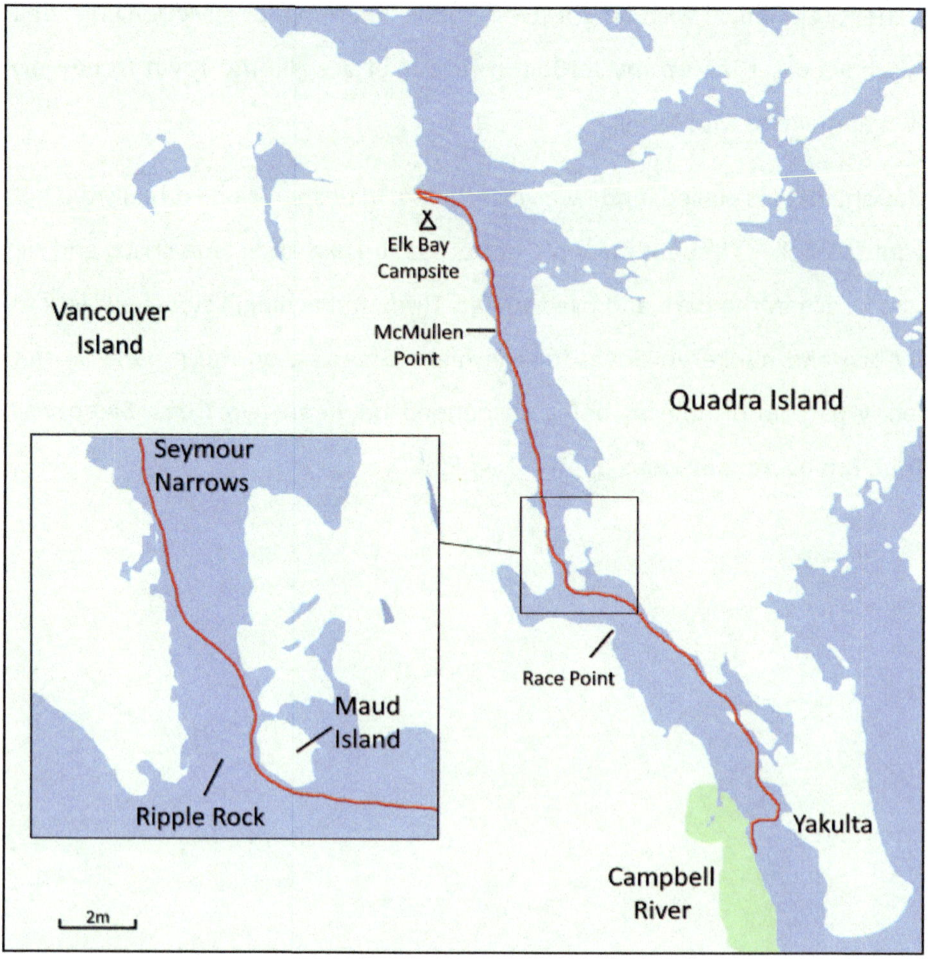

The rain woke me at five. Waking up on the ground made the muscle ache all the worse, as my sleeping mat really didn't provide any back or side support. I got out to find that Lilian had arrived and was also, amazingly, up. She'd managed to catch up, turning into the docks around midnight. I was impressed. Her resilience and endurance far outstripped mine to be able to deliver a performance like that to reel us in.

Dawn at Campbell River

We discussed the plan for Seymour Narrows, as that was today's challenge, obstacle, and all-round threat. The tide was flowing in from the North now, against us, and would continue to do so until slack at about eleven o'clock. All the conventional kayaking wisdom, and I'd read and heard plenty of this, recommended starting out from Campbell River three hours before slack, arriving just short of Ripple Rock just as slack arrived. There was a bay to the right where it was possible to lay up, and a causeway to the island opposite Ripple Rock that you could, if required, portage over and get back in, right in the Narrows.

Lilian headed off at seven to catch a flier, and I agreed I'd chase her down and meet her there at slack, and we'd paddle through together. Off she headed, while I began the laborious, now tedious, and frustrating packing process. It was tougher that morning to pack, given the drop off the dock to the boat, but I was at last becoming more proficient at it.

When is a hammock not a hammock? Bivi time at Campbell River

Tracker junkies were never far away. We had a visit from Al, who brought muffins for all of us for breakfast that I think his better half had made. Eating was becoming a real struggle. I had no appetite, but I knew I had to keep the calories piling in to keep the arms rotating. I retrieved my drysuit from the chain link fence separating us from the coastguard compound, along with the rest of my boat gear, kitted up and headed out.

I had a clear plan on a plate from Ian, and it began with a crossing to the East side of the channel. The current was on full flow against me. There was a point near the far bank where the arrow on my Garmin was actually pointing behind where I wanted to go, indicating that I was going backwards, such was the strength of the flow. It was a slog, keeping as close to shore as possible. At one point I ran over a submerged rock, and felt the hull buckle upwards as it ran down the underside. No, no, no! I had a temporary vision of a big hole and an ignominious premature end to the race, but Minnie held firm.

As I neared Seymour Narrows, the current began to slack, and I simultaneously hit the shelter of the bay alongside May Island. I fell into a lovely paddle groove, just as the media crew hove into view on their Zodiac.

> *"Hey y'all, er, we're just zipping around and it looks like... we're heading into Seymour Narrows and it looks like we have found a kayak contestant in Seymour Narrows, that goes by the name of Zen Dog. Now... Zen Dog has been winning the game against me for a while because he has, um, been disappearing every time I try to go see him, but uh, Rebecca, the other reporter Rebecca right there... was the hawk on watch, and was like 'look at that speck over there. I think it's Zen Dog' and I'm like 'ahh... you know there's kayakers out here too' and she's like 'GO. OVER. THERE. Shut up and go', and I was like 'all right' and, um, the further we went along, the better we felt that this was a good idea."*
>
> *"I don't know if we'll have a chance to talk because he is kind of positioning for... getting through the Narrows, and I don't wanna slow him down... It's a whole, like, different... there's different but same, know what I mean? Between those that just eschew all other power except human, go with the muscles, and really try and make it... oh yeah, I know, someone's commenting on the ninja stealth. I know that ninja stealth held out. Sadly, I think technology got the best of him, and absolute luck, because, I really, we had no idea where he was, because he keeps turning off his tracker or something."*

"He looks pretty dedicated. He hasn't even looked at us. We're not going to bother him too much. "

"Um, so he's setting up so y'all, I don't know if you've been tracking this, but around eleven o'clock is when the Narrows goes slack, and there's been what we thought were seven teams kinda set up to do that, uh, try and make the Narrows in the least evil times. Uh, one of the teams – Let's Row Maybe? ended up hitting the early morning and punching through, um, but the other teams look like they are still setting up, and Interstice somewhere around here as well, um... and it is... I mean it's the best time to do it. You know they get the slack, and... give it a little push on the other side."

"So he's still... I'm totally guessing right now, but he's still some number of miles out, something like four, If I look around, three and a half, three...we'll split it... three and a half miles out. Um and it is, what? Nine forty-six, so he wants it, you know, you want a stage, you want to get some play, you never want to hit it right at... You wanna get there a little bit early, you can do something else to wait a bit. You always want to hit it spot on. Maybe we'll try and get him after the pass, I'm hoping maybe on the other side. "

"Maybe I can ask him one question? I don't know. What do you think? Should I ask him a question?"

"Bob is all well? Is all well? Feeling good? Few little aches?"

"Says he has a few little aches, not too bad. He's a little taciturn this morning. I get it. OK, we're going to shut up. We'll see him hopefully up at the pass, too, at the Narrows."

(Daniel Evans – Transcript of "Zen Dog, Found Him!" Just past Gowlland Island)

It wasn't that I didn't want to talk to Daniel or the media guys at this stage. I was happy to chat with anyone, and it was a blast meeting all the tracker junkies on the way. It was just that, in the boat, it was nigh on impossible to hold a conversation and paddle, and I was on a mission that morning. Seymour Narrows had been built up into this big *thing*. There were the videos of the whirlpools, stories of powerboat drivers looking out their windows with their eyes at the same level as the water... "thank god I had a powerful engine to get out of that bugger." Well, I didn't have an engine, and this was a stretch I just wanted to tick off.

By ten thirty, I could see the island in front of Ripple Rock, and the small causeway that led out to it. Ripple Rock was famous for being blown up in the nineteen fifties to clear the way for larger vessels, in what was the largest non-nuclear detonation ever. I expected Lilian to be waiting at the causeway, or to be on the water on the far side. I rounded the island twenty minutes before slack tide. There was no current of note. I'd nailed the timing. I could not have been more relieved or happy. This was as well executed a morning as it could have been.

As I closed in on the inlet by the causeway, I saw Lilian pull out and row across the Narrows. I followed, and it probably took the best part of half an hour to reel her in. As we met up, Daniel and the media guys came alongside. I recall some self-congratulatory comments being exchanged about "no drama", and to be fair it was true. We were giving the R2AK team no headaches that day, even if my tracker was playing its usual silly buggers. We agreed a meet-up later that day, planning to get into Johnstone Strait, just beyond the Walkem Islands.

For the next hour or two we cleared the business end of the Narrows, chatting idly. With Lilian rowing, facing backwards, and me facing forwards, it was an easy way to have conversation just by tucking in behind, in her wake. We talked about her reasons for taking part, the race so far, and she probably suffered the first of my dad jokes. We'd not properly met, beyond the chats on Messenger and the text exchanges in the earlier stages of the race. She struck me as relaxed, easy-going, but underneath with that ultra-hard edge you'd expect of a soloist rower. In fact, she bore remarkable similarities to Marieke. It was strange and ironic to have lost one potential partner, and to then pick up another so alike.

Lilian in Seymour Narrows

Lilian had one luxury I did not. Every hour, for a few minutes, she would stop rowing, stand up, and stretch. Minnie didn't allow for this, and I still hadn't figured out why my butt was getting so cold. I needed my lunchtime break by the time we reached McMullen Point, but as we were now teamed, I curtailed it from hot food to nut butter bars and chocolate and took the opportunity to change my maps. I think the break was probably only fifteen minutes, and we were back on the water.

The VHF was pinging regularly. Mostly, it was calls from boaters, followed by interjections from the coastguard telling them to refrain from chatting on channel sixteen. There was a broadcast from another boat as we paddled out warning of orca coming through. We were now in *that* territory. I was hopeful they'd materialise, but sadly they kept their heads down.

I'd found over previous days that you paid for those breaks after lunch. It didn't take long for the fatigue to kick in, and the hour after lunch felt like a graveyard shift. For Lilian, having pulled such a long day the day before, that feeling must have been amplified. She called for a change of plan for the day, and I was only too happy to agree. To make the cut-off time in Ketchikan, my baseline distance for each day was set at thirty miles, and I'd averaged over forty so far, banking an extra day and a bit, so losing ten miles was no biggie. Add to this the murderous last few hours of the day before, and I was mentally ready for a break. Elk Bay was up ahead, and we plumped for camping there.

As we rowed and paddled into the bay there was a shout from Lilian. She'd spotted a school of porpoises behind me. There were plenty of them, but I was feeling too tired to turn my boat around to watch properly. Watching their dorsal fins rising and falling in patterns over my shoulder, it was still quite a sight.

We had a debate as to where to camp. There was clearly a logging operation going on to our left, and up ahead looked good to me. Lilian favoured what looked to be a proper campsite on our left. We got halfway over the bay before we opted for Lilian's choice, but we stupidly decided not to paddle all the way to the campsite - my fault - stopping a few hundred metres short so I could find a hammock spot. In the event the campsite catered for tents and hammocks, and we ended up ferrying gear back and forth between boats and pitches, at far more of a distance than we should have left. Hindsight is a wonderful thing. Another time, and we'd have landed right in front of the campground.

The big bonus of disembarking with Lilian was her boat roller. I'd never seen one before. An inflatable sausage-shaped canvas bag, you tucked it under one end of the boat, and you could roll the vessel, not entirely unladen, up or down the beach on your own. You could manage what felt like three boat lengths in one hit, taking loads of the grunt out of the worst two exercises of the day. This was an economy of scale from the partnership I'd not foreseen, and it was to be a bonus at every stop and start to come. I definitely had boat roller envy.

We set up, and Lilian went to catch some zeds. I found the stream and took the opportunity to have a shave. Then, fetching my first aid kit from my boat, I took the opportunity to deal with my hands. I now had plenty of blisters, and the skin on my hands was turning white from the constant contact with the salt water. The dissolving callouses were now falling off, leaving craters where they'd been, right in the crooks of my fingers. It stung like hell, applying the ointment, and I swear it felt worse than before having treated them.

After we'd eaten and had a pow-wow about the following day's plan, I was ready to hoist my food. There was a convenient bar between two trees, and there was none of the English amateurism of three days before. The bag, with rope attached, went over second time, and the food was safely stashed. Not that it was likely to be a problem. There were plenty of campers there, and the general consensus was that we were safe from bears for tonight at least.

I think we forfeit three to four hours that day, but it was worth it. We set alarms for stupid o'clock the following morning and hit the sack. With Ian's guidance, I felt like we'd outsmarted one of the biggest beasts of the race, making it seem as tame as a pussy cat. I had company going forward, and that took the edge off the challenges to come. Tomorrow I'd be closing in on the patch of water I knew. I went to sleep in a happy place.

Day Six : Elk Bay to the Broken Islands – 47 miles

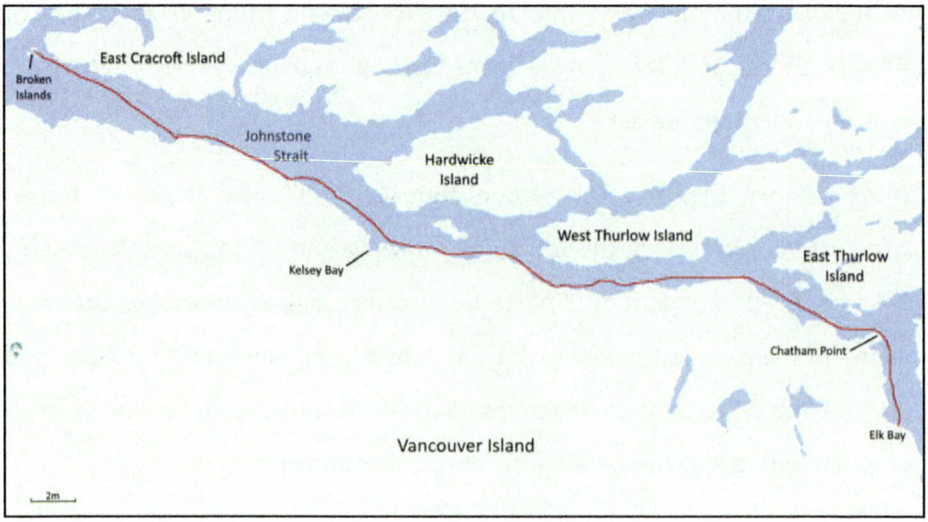

Three-thirty arrived too early. I broke camp in the dark and relayed my gear to Minnie down the beach. Watching Lilian doing the same but far more efficiently made me regret my lack of slickness, not least having had to retrieve my torch from my buoyancy aid in the pitch black at the boat where I'd left it before starting. We rolled the boats to the water and were off by five thirty. It was beginning to get light, but we left our navigation lights on so that we could be seen.

It didn't take us long to clear Rock Bay and make the turn into Johnstone Strait. It was raining and we had a tailwind, and I was feeling all right, save for the freezer under my backside and the feeling that the padding sat on that foam was not providing the comfort of the first week. Just after the corner, I put in to change maps and sort out my drinking hose. By the time I'd finished faffing with these tasks, Lilian was almost out of sight. It took the best part of an hour to reel her back in.

Entering Johnstone Strait at dawn.

By the time we approached the end of West Thurlow Island the wind was beginning to pick up behind us and I could feel the ebbing tide underneath helping us on. It was not as welcome as I'd have wanted, as the waves were beginning to swell. Around Palmer Bay, I decided to step out from the shore a little and make the most of the tailwind, not least to catch up on Lilian. I was regretting that twenty minutes later, as I could feel the wind trying to edge me further towards the middle of the strait, and away from the close comfort of shore. It was a minor repeat of the conditions on the first day of the first leg. The latency of the effects of your decisions came sharply back into focus. I worked my way carefully back in nearer to shore, foregoing the promise of speed for the confidence of safety.

We made it to Ripple Shoal at the end of West Thurlow just after eleven o'clock. Ripple Shoal marks a confluence of Johnstone Strait and Chancellor

Channel, so we carefully stuck to the south shore to avoid the tidal races further out. Lilian was taking her breaks on the hour, and I was stopping and eating at the same time. As we were now teamed up, and because Johnstone Strait was not offering the inviting beaches we'd had up until now, and because it was raining, we did not stop for a beach lunch. With hindsight, this may have been a mistake. The hour to stretch and eat something other than Clif and chocolate bars was something I'd got used to, and although there was the inevitable post-lunch malaise back in the boat, the revitalisation definitely had paid dividends on the previous days.

By mid-afternoon I was beginning to flag. I put in at St Vincent Bight just before three o'clock as by then I really needed to stretch out and catch a bit of a break. Sitting in the boat without paddling was not cutting it. Progress was feeling painfully slow, even if the Garmin was still indicating a general speed of over four knots. In my head I'd expected us to get to Robson Bight that afternoon, and be near the end of Johnstone Strait that evening. I think because I wasn't meeting those expectations my head was beginning to drop a bit. It didn't help that I was yawning almost constantly. Well short of Robson Bight, Lilian made the call to cross the Strait, which was a break from my planned route, and we took a bearing into the wet mist towards the North shore.

We made it to the Broken Islands just before five o'clock. The weather and the cumulation of the race so far made it the hardest day to date. I was figuring in my head that there was a pattern emerging. I'd have a really good day followed by one where - by the end of it - I'd be dead on my feet. We skirted right around the main island in the chain, finally locating the beach that looked like the one by the campsite. Once the boats were up, we went in search of the pitch points. It wasn't easy. There were several large tree trunks, side by side, which we had to work our way over and into the wood. That involved passing bags over each one, clambering over, and repeating, all without slipping and causing ourselves mischief.

The campsite itself was merely a few square metres under the tree canopy. There was just enough space to sling the hammock, and for Lilian to set her tent. We both set up our tarpaulins because it was relentlessly chucking it down. My set-up felt ragged, unprofessional, and borderline inadequate in the rain. There were guy lines going here, there, and everywhere, carabiner-ed to trees, tied off to saplings. My tarpaulin barely protected the hammock from the droplets coming down. I set up a groundsheet to sit on and, shivering, cooked up my food. There didn't appear to be any sign of bears, which was just as well because - and I regret this with hindsight – I barely bothered to follow best practice, and we both ate our food by our sleeping arrangements, a general no-no.

We laid a plan for the following day. We'd carry on down the Strait, and then at Cracroft Point make a turn up towards the mainland. For all the fatigue, it felt to me like we had nailed another section of the race in Johnstone, or at least we would have done by the close of the next stint. I crawled into my sleeping bag at about six thirty, knowing that we'd be up at sparrows again in the morning.

By nine o'clock I was awake again. The cold was seeping through the sleeping bag and sapping the heat out of me. I unzipped the hammock and hauled in my clothes dry sack which was on the groundsheet just underneath me. I put on another thermal top and my puffer jacket and shed my damp leggings in favour of dry ones. This was no mean feat as I had no intention of leaving hammock, the whole thing rocking as I manoeuvred myself into my additional clothes. Yet it was still a miserably cold night and I slept fitfully, for the first time not really looking forward to getting up and back at it in the morning.

Day Seven : Broken Islands to Lagoon Cove – 21 miles

We have a problem

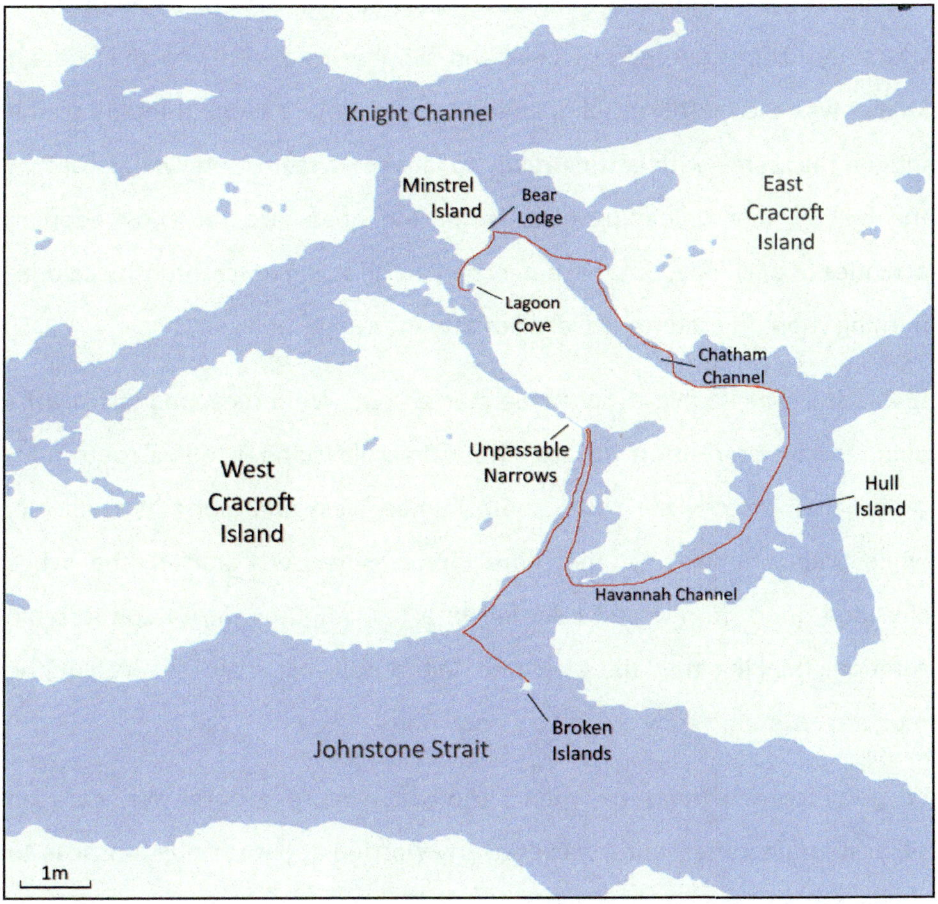

It was as if I'd not been to sleep. It was a restless night, punctuated by the heat leeching out of my sleeping bag, through the insulation mat wedged between the hammock layers, and out into the mist. It was the first night and morning of the trip where it had been raining solidly, and the damp added to the cold. I felt clammy as I put my wet clothes back on, and then the drysuit. I tried to make my breakfast bar more palatable and easier to swallow by watering it into a gruel, but it just made me gag on each mouthful.

It must have been a feeling of wanting to keep up with the Joneses, for it felt like a race to get everything down, bagged, and back over the obstacle course of lichen-covered branches and slippery tree trunks to the boats. I knew I was the inefficient one, and the pressure just seemed to add to the fatigue that came with getting ready to launch. It seems totally illogical that the loading and unloading process for the boats are the most sapping activities of each day, but there it is: half an hour of higher intensity calorie-burning chore in order to travel all of fifty metres.

It was still dark at five thirty as we started out. We'd recapped last night's plan, and we started off towards West Cracroft Island. I took a route that, rather than directly cut to its shore, aimed west and along its coastline, while Lilian plumped for the more direct route. As I started, the aches subsided quite quickly and I settled in a few minutes into a comfortable rotation, thinking that the alternate "good day, bad day" theory cut the mustard after all. Today could be a good one.

I'd got fifteen minutes in when I thought I heard a horn. We were on separate trajectories, and I wasn't overly worried about sticking too close to Lilian that morning, and I wasn't about to get left behind at a distance where I would spend another hour catching up with her. I was sure that had sapped me the morning before. A minute later, I heard it again. It wasn't something I could ignore. I picked up my VHF to find the batteries had gone, which was entirely my fault for not checking and it left me no option but to turn back and find out what, if anything, had happened. I wasn't about to repeat the coastguard incident with Oaracle from a few days before.

It took me fifteen minutes to get back, and it wasn't without the frustration in my head of not progressing towards Ketchikan, going backwards, not forwards. It was ten of those minutes before I could pick out Lilian from the waves. As I pulled up alongside, she told me that the conditions really weren't good for a rowing boat in the Straits, and she wanted to try another route. This was an absolutely fair sentiment. I could only imagine that some of the previous days, particularly offshore from French Creek, would have been really hard given that she'd have no forward visibility of the waves, save what she could see in the rear-view mirror mounted on her boat mast.

We pulled out the maps to have a look at alternatives. Here, I was out of scope on my paper maps, as my route had steadfastly stuck to the main strait, and there was no contingency or printout of the channels to our North. On my route we weren't even supposed to be at the Broken Islands; we should still have been south on the Vancouver Island shore. We looked at Lilian's chart. If we paddled and rowed north, there was a narrow channel through to Lagoon Cove just under four miles away. If we could make that, then we could slip the boats through the creek to the inlet on the other side and resume our trip in Knight Inlet on the other side. This would position us well to get close to the channels leading over to the mainland. The plan for the day was around twenty-five miles, given the forecast and especially the wind, and I was in complete agreement with the cut-through variation. We agreed and set out towards Port Harvey and the short cut.

An hour later we got there, and our hearts sank. Where the creek was marked, there was a rickety old gangway, and a load of brush, and not a sign of any water. If there had been a way through, it was now overgrown with bushes, trees, and undergrowth. There was no question of getting through. Lilian was unnecessarily apologetic. It wasn't her decision alone; I'd signed up for it too and we'd both cocked up. The question was: what to do to carry on? There was back to Johnstone, or another route around between the Cracroft islands in a channel, wider than this one, but still a funnel. The choices weren't good. I knew Lilian wouldn't go for Johnstone, and the tide was turning, meaning we were going to have a battle to get through the channels. Reluctantly I agreed to the latter. We retraced our steps and turned east away from where we should be going.

As in any activity, work, home, or sporting, your frame of mind, your mood, can have a great impact on how your day progresses and how you perform. The previous day had definitely battered me, and the deviation to our plan that morning had added uncertainty to my head. Not having a map in front of me with a nice pink line on it to follow, and no clear destination at the end of it, was another gut punch. To make the navigational mistake that we made was a hammer blow, swiftly followed by another one from the knowledge that that cock-up was going to cost us a lot of extra effort paddling against the tide. There was no choice but to dig in, but that morning I went from feeling in control of what I was doing to the sensation that I'd lost it. On its own, that change in mental state doubled the feeling of the energy I was having to expend that day. My head was dropping. The confidence I had until then went absent.

The trick usually is to compartmentalise the race, to split the good and bad days apart, and scratch out the bad ones when they are done. It's possible to break it down further into mornings or afternoons, but the simplest approach here is just to set a target of the next bay, the next corner, or the end of the next hour, tick it off and then grind out the next one. Then, at the end of the day, you can say to yourself "I did twenty five miles today, and now the total distance for the trip is x hundred done." The hope for the end of this day was to be able to say: "I've cleared Vancouver Island, and I'm on to the next stretch." Two and a half miles back to the turn, another two to the next point. I was beginning to recover some of my mojo as I went down the channel, even though our speed was nearer three knots than four. It didn't feel like a channel, it was still so wide down there, and the rain now gave way to sun. I was still feeling the cumulative effects of the miles and days before, but I was ticking off the markers, and ticking off the hours.

As we approached Hadley Bay, I began lobbying for a break, or more precisely looking for an excuse for one. My Garmin batteries needed changing, as did the VHF ones, and we'd been underway for nearly four hours. We were about to hit Chatham Channel, right on the nose of the tide. Chatham was less than a couple of hundred metres wide and it was clear that paddling into it would be like paddling upstream in a fast-flowing river. The sides were relatively straight, meaning that, at best, there would be only narrow eddies to work against the current in, if any eddies at all.

Our break was nearly half an hour. I think Lilian was taking pity on me by this point. The blisters on my right hand were sore but manageable. The ones on my left hand were worse, and it looked like the tiny cuts on the ends of my little and ring fingers had become infected. I was unable to close either of them onto the paddle shaft when holding it. The upshot was that there was a load transfer into my wrist muscles, the ones running down the inside of my forearm, and I could now feel the beginnings of tendonitis. It was one of my worst fears, up there with the bears and the sea conditions. What we were about to head in to was going to really test things to the full.

As we headed up the channel our speed was nearly down to two knots, half what I'd been averaging, and meaning I was losing half my input to the tide. I was hugging the shore, but this was creating a new problem I'd not yet faced. There were plenty of submerged rocks, and Minnie was now regularly scraping over them. A hole in her hull would be the end of the adventure, and it was toe-curling every time I felt the sandpapery surfaces screech down the hull. In an ideal world I'd be far enough out that this was not a problem, but there would be no headway against the tide without it.

We made less than two miles in the next half an hour, and I called another break. I could no longer see the sense in carrying on until the tide changed, yet we were stuck in a channel where there was precious little space for me to get out, let alone for Lilian. She was outgunning me for strength and stamina and remaining really rather chipper at the same time. As I got back in and we headed off, we crossed to the East Island and picked our way up the shore. Just before twelve, and less than three miles on, we made what was almost a beach, which was under the full onslaught of the incoming waves, and managed to land in the shelter of a small rock. I was all for stopping for the day, but Lilian persisted, rightly, reasoning that there was a resort just up ahead, almost in sight. We should aim for it, given that it would make a better proposition for camping compared to the sliver of inhospitable shingle we were on.

We battled our way over to Minstrel Island. There was a lodge just above a marina and a beach beyond. We made it to the beach, leaving the boats close to the water's edge. I laid out my wet gear to dry. Lilian found an old camp chair, I an old buoy to sit on - she definitely scavenged the better seating deal - and we settled down for a while to recharge. I was spent for the day and hoping for a major recharge for moving on tomorrow and had no intention of going further.

After a while we went exploring the paths into the brush close by, bear spray in hand, to see if we could make it round to the lodge. There were salmonberries in the bushes and Lilian, more savvy about wild plants than I, told me they were edible. I doubt I'd have trusted myself to eat them if I was left to my own ignorance. When the path ran out, we tried to get to the house, successfully this time. For once I was the one who spotted the otter make a dash over the rocks for shelter in the trees.

We - well, maybe Lilian – decided to approach the lodge inhabitants to see if we could pitch on their lawn. It was considerably more inviting than the beach we were parked on. We knocked and found a lady working inside, and I let Lilian do the talking. What began as a suspicious and almost defensive conversation soon changed into a more hospitable one, and soon she'd agreed to the idea of us staying on the lawn for the night, and we were off to the boats.

There was another lady repainting the pontoon as we came back, and we were in the process of unloading the boats and heading up to set up camp when the media crew turned up in their Zodiac. It was a relief to see friendly faces, especially Rebecca. I showed her my hands. Now one of the callouses on my left hand was completely dissolved off to add to my woes. I was hoping hard that it would follow the callous on my right hand, which had set over and was no longer causing me major pain. As we talked, it became clear that they were staying at Lagoon Cove, a mere mile from where we were. While staying at the Bear Lodge had its appeal, not least the appeal of not going anywhere else that day, the thought of being with friendly faces that evening was just enough to persuade me to put my drysuit back on, repack the boat, and at half past four to slog the remaining mile to the Marina.

It was a glorious sunny evening as we moored up and decamped onto the dock. The operators at the cove kindly let us tie up on the inside of the gangway, and we gradually set up camp right there. There were clearly a lot of bears in the vicinity, and we were strongly discouraged from moving away from the water. There were toilets, a basic luxury, and a table and benches where we were able to set up and cook. Tantalisingly, there was a shop with an ice cream freezer just outside, and I treated myself to two cornets, which my stomach paid dearly for the next day.

Alongside Rebecca was Lynette, another journalist who had clearly struck up a rapport with Lilian. I think she'd interviewed Lilian before. Although we'd had few snatched opportunities for conversation during the race, I guess I had forged more of a friendship with Rebecca, and I'd barely met Lynette before; just the one encounter off Comox Point. It was probably the worst time to try and kick off a dialogue with me. I was motivationally bankrupt that evening. I tried briefly to explain the difficulties I was having with my hands to Lynette, barely registering that she was filming. It may have come over as a Great British whinge, which was probably a fair reflection of the low I was at. Then, as we sat at the table trying to replenish the calories, the marina operators produced a magnificent tray of prawns. For a seafood gourmet they must have looked top notch, but for a fish philistine like me it was a generous but wasted gesture. I think Lilian did pretty well on the servings from that.

I'd had it. I would have to try and recharge with sleep to have any chance of a good paddle in the morning. Given we were looking at a three o'clock start, and a one thirty wake-up, that sleep had to be now. I quietly took myself off to my bivi and lay down. When Lynette appeared shortly after I made my apologies. Nobody wants to see a miserable Brit on camera, and she kindly left me to myself.

I couldn't sleep and my left hand was killing me, both the open blisters where the callouses had been and the finger cuts. At about ten, I got up with the intent to find some disinfectant to apply to them. Rebecca was still up, and she helped me try and locate some, first in the media boat, and then with success on one of the cruisers moored up in the marina. You could see the cuts foaming away as we soaked them. I think about now the switch was flipping in my head. It had been a day of bad decisions and bad luck. I'd stupidly let it get on top of me, but underneath all of that I knew I had a major, critical problem. I crawled back into my bivi and spent the next few restless hours coming to terms with the decision that was making itself.

The rationale was straightforward. We were coming up to the most exposed stretch of coast up to and beyond Cape Caution. We already had minimal cover for rescue or extraction, and that had been the case ever since we left Campbell River, a hundred miles further back. The cuts were a problem, and if the tendonitis in my wrist deteriorated further, and there was every indication it would, then I was not only making it a lot harder for myself to get out, but also very awkward for anyone to come in and bail me out. Everything pointed to pulling out now.

Lilian tapped on the canvas at half one, and it didn't take long to explain where I was at, and that I was done. She went back to sleep, justifiably not keen on setting off alone in the dark. She'd quietly left when I woke up in the morning. I cannot remember exactly when I bumped into Rebecca, but that was the moment that I really scratched. She went in search of ideas to get out – I was still contemplating a paddle over to Port McNeill on Vancouver Island at that stage – while I found a very hospitable boat owner who shared a cuppa and a conversation for a while.

Fortuitously, Rebecca and the media crew found me a ride out. There was a boat, with a kayak rack on its side, heading for Port Hardy on Vancouver Island, but leaving immediately. Everything gets rushed in my memory around this time. I frantically packed the Ikea bags with my gear, and my boat was loaded onto the kayak rack for me. I ditched much of the food there; the media crew kindly volunteered to dispose of it for me. It felt like an incredible waste. I also left them with the memory foam seat, and as I extracted it from its dry bag, the cause of my cold backside over the last few days became clear. The bag had leaked, and the foam was saturated with freezing cold water. It had been like sitting on ice cubes for those days, and this was a lesson learned too late. I do remember Rebecca crying, and that rammed home just how invested those who were involved around us had become in what we were trying to do. With hardly a chance to say goodbye and thanks to anyone, I was on board Knot Fast, and headed out. My time in the race was over.

Field Report: Lagoon Cove: A Forced Perspective of Beauty and Community

June 25, 2022 By Rebecca Ross, Field Reporter

As the Race to Alaska continues for many, so does the film crew's chase to track down racers to photograph and interview. On board a 44' steel Diesel Duck named Seaducktress, we make our way through Queen Charlotte Strait and catch up with Teams Don't Tell Mom and Let's Row Maybe?. The two teams are focused as they fight against the choppy currents.

From there, we progress through Broughton Archipelago towards a full-service marina in Lagoon Cove on East Cracroft Island. For hours, we're graced by islands chock full of lush green conifers while larger snow-peaked mountains loom in the background. A sight I have never seen before and recall many racers looking forward to camping in the area.

Proceeding towards the marina, Peter Geerlofs, a member of the Northwest Maritime Center board of directors and our R2AK volunteer captain, puts Seaducktress into neutral, but instead, the engine dies. Unable to restart the engine, he thinks fast and scrambles to drop the anchor to save a 37-ton boat from helplessly drifting into the dock. After being safely moored to the dock with the help of Dan and Kelly, the new marina owners, we try to settle our nerves.

But the race stops for no one, not even for a film crew on a broken boat. Adhering to the plan, we hop in a dinghy and speed off towards solo paddlers and rowers, Zen Dog and Interstice, aiming to intercept them before they settle on a nearby private island just minutes away. After briefly chatting with the two teams and describing Lagoon Cove, they swiftly decide to relocate to our lovely neck of the woods so we can get our stories there.

Before departing, I ask Bob how he's holding up. "I feel battered," he replied, showcasing his hands riddled with thick calluses and burgundy-colored blisters. He confides that he had changed his paddling style to relieve the pain in his hands, and now his overworked wrists are hurting—a sheer lose-lose situation. Seeing the obvious pain he's endured, I realize the choice to paddle another few miles must feel like paddling a hundred for Bob.

Everyone reconvenes at Lagoon Cove, the sun starting to settle and the harsh light softening to a soft, warm glow, yet the marina remains full of excitement. Even Lillian extends her 6 pm curfew to mingle with new faces and provide more stories for the familiar Race to Alaska field reporters.

Despite being an incredibly remote island, East Cracroft brims with community and support for mariners, race film crew, and exhausted teams. Kelly and Dan generously contribute to the welcome vibe of the island by hosting a daily "potluck happy hour" where boaters come together with a dish and feast on the patio in front of the workshop adorned by a 20-year collection of boat flags. It feels effortless getting caught up in the increasingly endless northern summer light.

As the night eventually comes to an end and I begin to get settled on the boat, I hear Bob's voice nearby. When I ask what is going on, Bob simply shows me his hands. I might as well be looking at rigor mortis–his stiff fingers splay open, unable to close, let alone grip a paddle. A look of deep worry is on his face. As for me, my heart starts to sink—Oh no, Bob! Compelled to help, we rummage through the boat for a first aid kit but find nothing. I search around the marina, still nothing. Finally, I tap on a yacht nearby with its lights still on. In a panic, I had trouble even putting words to the situation, so instead, I point to Bob's hands in desperation.

I pace up and down the dock outside the good samaritan's yacht, waiting for the verdict and wishing for a miracle. Moments later, Bob comes out with newly disinfected hands, but nothing else has changed. It doesn't feel like enough, but I hold my tongue and keep my thoughts to myself—This isn't good!

"I don't know what to do," Bob says. My thoughts are shouting, No! No! No! No! He's come too far to be stopped like this. "Can you stay a day and let your hand heal?" I suggest as warm tears start to cloud my vision.

Bob looks at me and hugs me, "We are all in this—you too!" Now I can feel the tears on my cheeks. I continue to walk back with Bob to his camp spot, his bivy next to Lillian's tent on the dock. They've been recently sharing the journey ever since Seymour Narrows and have had plans to continue together. "The problem is, if I stay, I will lose Lillian," Bob whispers. "And if I go, I put myself at risk of being unable to turn around." I understand his dilemma, but still, I tell myself, Don't cry! Don't cry! Both of us emotional, Bob assures us both that it's not over until it's over.

Only slightly consoled, a part of me knows he can't continue in his state. As Bob retires for the night, I stand looking out from the dock with enough gentle ambient light to see the islands dotted across the rustling waters of the cove. In that moment, I recall a story he told me back at Dungeness Spit while I strained my ears over the wind. He told me how people are usually focused on the finish line and by doing so, they pass the beauty that happens all around them. Instead, he wanted to make sure he treasured those moments.

The following day I awake to the sound of commotion. I see Bob packing his things—Lillian of Team Interstice already long gone. With Bob's hands unimproved since I saw them last, he had decided to pull out of the race. Bitter, yet fortunate timing. If he hadn't transitioned over to Lagoon Cove, a volunteer wouldn't have been able to offer him a ride to Port Hardy, giving his destroyed hands a merciful break.

And overall, if it hadn't been for Race to Alaska, I would never have known this place existed, let alone seen it in person. And if I hadn't remembered Bob's advice and gotten stuck at Lagoon Cove with moments of forced downtime with wonderful people, I wouldn't have taken the time to fully enjoy these beautiful moments.

Aftermath

Resurfacing

I believe in the future. It is wonderful because it stands on what has been achieved.

I felt like I'd had my boat snatched from under me, and I was in shock at what had just happened. I never really felt like I made the decision to retire. The series of events and the situation I was in made it for me. I sat in the cabin at the table, and didn't really know how to take it in.

With the Knot Fast crew. Derrill, Shelley and Bob. Jamie was on camera duty.

I was on Jamie's boat, Knot First, and he was crewed by Bob, Shelley and Derrill. Derrill was a nurse, and he looked at my hands. I'd figured I would have to get them looked at by a doctor. His verdict was that I needed to keep them away from salt water for a while, and they would gradually return to normal.

They were the most generous hosts and companions for the trip back. They were on their way north, but to my great good luck were making a stopover in Port Hardy on the way. I was fed and looked after generously. I spent some of the time talking through my decision with Helen and organising the aftermath further south with her. There was still a gap to fill from Hardy to Seattle, and that would have to wait for getting back on land. I'd originally thought it would be possible to take a ferry back down the Inside Passage, but this no longer ran and was therefore not an option.

I'd asked Ian about scratch plans back in the early exchanges we'd had, and he'd just replied that there would be plenty of help, and not to worry about it. I hadn't really believed him, but he was already, yet again, proving to be right. I'd lucked in on Jamie and Knot First. When we arrived in Port Hardy it took very little time to organise the next stage, back down to Nanaimo with Larry Roy, an old friend from years ago who had guided me and my wife on our first wilderness paddle from Telegraph Cove, just south of Port McNeill.

I'd figured on getting to Victoria and back over to Olympia, but at this point Lilian remotely intervened. She organised Dave, her other half, to help me out. I'm still under the impression that he would have driven all the way up to Port Hardy to get me if I hadn't been able to get down to Nanaimo. As it was, Larry generously put me up for a night and then drove me to the ferry terminal at Nanaimo, supplying me with a set of wheels to get the boat on and off. Dave went above and beyond and collected me in Tsawwassen, drove me over the border to Seattle, and then put me up and put up with me for four days. The whole extraction from Lagoon Cove to Seattle took less than three days. I am indebted to all the parties who generously and selflessly helped me out in this time.

With Larry at Nanaimo.

My race might have been over, but R2AK certainly wasn't, and I had too much invested to just walk away. All of the human-powered crews and plenty of solos were still out there, pounding their way up towards Ketchikan, and the tracker junkie in me was back in full swing, galvanised by knowing the guys pulling the oars and the paddles. Watching the head-to-head showdown between Don't Tell Mom and Let's Row Maybe? come to a superbly tense finale was immense, the ladies from Maine pipping the Olympian powerhouse by less than a day. Could I ever doubt that Ian and Janice would bring Oaracle home for yet another R2AK finish? All three of these crews were home in under eighteen days, in time to catch a ferry together back down to Seattle. And then there was still Lilian.

I guess I put all of my eggs into one basket when I scratched in out-and-out wanting someone to finish, and that was Lilian. It was funny, because one of the conversations we had, I think on that rainy day paddling along Johnstone Strait, was about finishing. It was fairly clear to me that Lilian had painted a big target on my back and wanted to beat me, but conversely, I couldn't give a rat's backside about beating her. During that exchange, I told her she could have the finish ahead of me, either by a whisker, or a finish alone; I could stop for a shave or something for a while and let her have a moment in Ketchikan to herself. Now that I was out, in my head, her making it became super-important.

She made it past Cape Caution and to Bella Bella, but by this point her mindset wasn't great. As I was staying with Dave, I was party to some of the exchanges between them on where she was at, and in Bella Bella the strain of being alone was definitely taking its toll on her. I tried to help by sending maps and pushing the positivity, but it was not enough. While I understand and respect her decision to withdraw, for me it was another blow. Lilian is about the toughest racer I have ever met. This will not be popular with her, but I was quite mad at her for pulling out because I felt that, once she'd made it to Bella Bella, she'd broken the back of the race. Physically she had it. Technically she had it. The difficulty was being alone. Looking back, it's ironic that I had the wobbles mentally in Victoria, while she was a rock, only for the situation to turn on its head in the first few days of the second stage. By Campbell River I was comfortable in my own company, and fairly confident in my limited abilities to deal with what was to come. Would that have changed around Cape Caution? We will never know the answer to that. Regardless, she was the strongest solo in the race that year by a country mile or ten. I desperately wanted her to finish. For her. For us, the little guys. I was gutted when she withdrew.

How do you process taking part in something like the R2AK, and then having to retire from it? It is a brutal event, of that there is no question. For the two weeks after pulling out, there were times in each day where I just could not stay awake. Driving around Seattle, I found myself apologising to Dave just before passing out in the passenger seat of his car, unable to remain conscious. I took a road trip with Helen and Steve, with Minnie on the roof, all the way back to their place in Denver. Without fail each morning and each afternoon in the car I'd be spark-o. Helen, needless to say, shamelessly took full advantage and plenty of pictures of me catching flies. Three weeks later, when I finally arrived home, I weighed myself to find I was nine kilos – a stone and a quarter - lighter than when I'd headed out to the start.

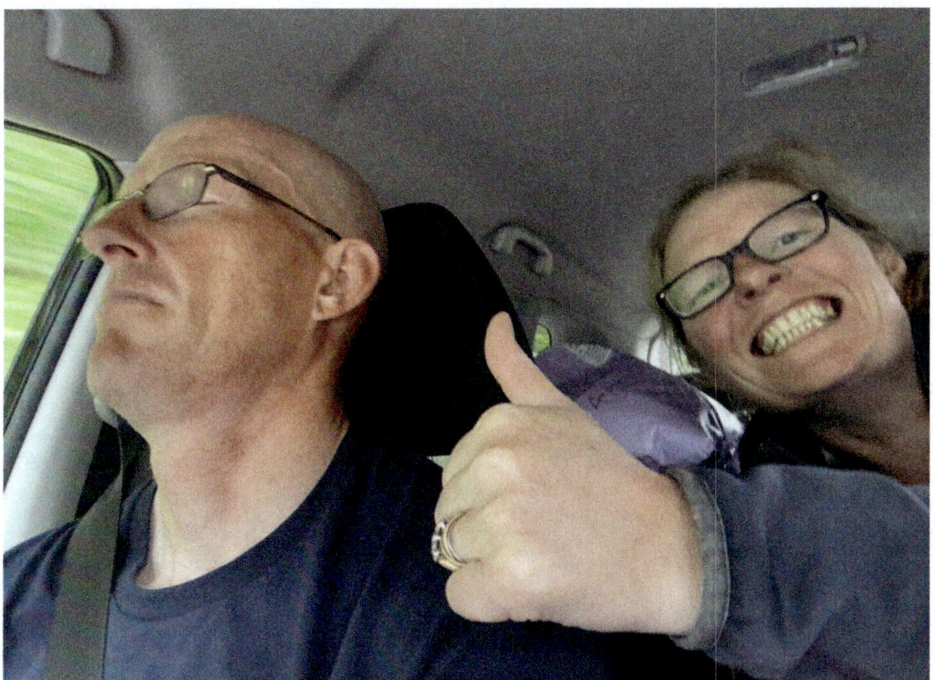

Thank you cuz. Courtesy, kind of, Helen Green

In that time, on the trip down the island and the road trip, I was trying to come to terms with how it ended. It was hard to look at my endeavour and see anything but a failure. The goal was to get to Ketchikan, and that box wasn't ticked. I had not made it to Cape Caution, not seen Dixon Entrance, and not paddled up Princess Royal of Grenville Channels. I hadn't even made it halfway.

My hands took a month to heal. I could still see traces of the damage when I arrived back in England. It's been the thing people have asked about the most since the race, replacing the "what about the bears" question I repeatedly got beforehand. They were blisters, and blisters repair. The infection was gone in three days, just as Derrill had predicted. There has been no lasting damage to my tendons, and I am back paddling, and looking forward.

Making sense of how and why I scratched has taken longer. It is only writing about the race that is really clearing things up in my head, and it is not something that sits well with me. As I relived the last day, whole chunks of memory came back to the fore. I had blotted out the memories of paddling back out of the dead end and into the narrow channel, blanked the mental hammering I'd taken from the knowledge we'd cocked up our decisions and that we were going to pay for it. The blisters and the infection are only part of the scratching story. I buckled that day. Did I give in too easily? I suspect that the physical issues I had would have done for me a few days further on, but there is no denying that my head got the better of me at Lagoon Cove. Now, months on, I still have no regrets about my decision, and only a few about not making it further, not making it to Ketchikan.

There were two events that helped to bring things back into perspective. As Helen, Steve and I neared the end of the road trip to Denver, we stopped on the last evening at a pizzeria in Glenwood Springs, Colorado, a good thousand miles plus from where the race had begun. It wasn't even our first-choice restaurant, the threat of thunderstorms having closed the outside eating space in our first choice and meaning we had to relocate for Helen's dogs' sake. I'd reached the last of my cleanish clothes, and the only t-shirt I had left was the R2AK race shirt. I'd been reluctant to wear it, because I didn't feel I merited that privilege, such were my feelings about where I was at.

As we waited for our food to arrive, this guy walks over and asks: "Were you in the race?" When I answered "Yes", he asked me which team I was. I told him "Zen Dog ". "I was in Team Elsewhere", he replied. "We came second. We won the steak knives." Cue Josiah, who was sat at a table not ten yards from us. He was with his Antipodean girlfriend, Angie, and his mother, and they quickly relocated to our table, and we spent the evening talking over the race. It was really the conversation with Angie that began to put things into perspective:

"We were following Josiah and Elsewhere, but there wasn't really that much going on with them, but you guys, you lot at the back. Juan de Fuca Strait. Seymour Narrows. You rocked. You guys were awesome!"

Perspective. I was still out paddling when Josiah and Elsewhere had already finished. Yes, the main goal eluded me. I had missed out on some of the race, but some of the sections I had completed stood up as major achievements in their own right. Yes, Juan de Fuca. Yes, Seymour Narrows. Georgia Strait, Johnstone, yes, yes... and Edward Monkton was right. I needed not to forget that. Rebecca hadn't in her write-up of Dungeness, nor in that last night's unfolding, a piece of journalism that was accurate, sympathetic, and for which I am truly grateful. It isn't the destination, but it is the glory of the ride, and the ride was indeed glorious.

Zen Dog meets Team Elsewhere. Courtesy Helen Green

Yet it was more than any personal achievement, partial or otherwise. R2AK is an ingenious device and Jake, its father, its instigator, has come up with something truly wonderful. Race to Alaska is not so much a story about boats. It is a story about people. It is a story about the kindness of strangers. It brings people together in a more intensely brilliant way than any other event I can think of. The racers I met, to a man and to a woman, epitomised the best of what sport should exhibit. There is no gamesmanship in R2AK, far from it. The help I had, shared purpose and sense of community I felt with these crews, especially us little guys at the back, still brings a smile to my face when I look back. The tracker junkies though: if as racers we rocked, these guys were the crowd that roared. Now, when I talk about the race, it's about meeting Patrick and Peg, Diane, Liz... It's easy in day-to-day life, especially in a working environment where people with their own agendas rub up against each other, to get dragged down. R2AK brings the best out in people and reaffirms how awesome we can be. All of this came flooding back as I talked through my encounters with Angie and Josiah. It was impossible not to start floating on those experiences again.

The second event that helped me make my peace with R2AK 2022 came on the flight home from Vancouver a week later. I was sat in the window seat on the port side of the plane, and we took off to the west, heading over the sea and temporarily in the opposite direction to home. It was a clear evening, and I looked out south over the San Juan and the Gulf Islands. We must have made about ten thousand feet, but I could not see as far south as Juan de Fuca; the wider body of water I was expecting was just too far away. Then, as the plane turned north and then east, I was able to look down on Georgia Strait. I could make out Gabriola Island, Nanaimo, Denman Island, all the way up towards, but not quite to, Campbell River. I could virtually identify my camping stops along the way I'd paddled all of this, and I could see miles and miles, and yet I couldn't see where I'd begun, and I certainly couldn't see where it had ended for me. Another perspective, a bird's eye one.

There were already a number of things in motion by the time I was on that plane out of Vancouver. I'd already reached out to Doug Shoop and offered my services as crew, should he want someone to persevere with the following year. I'd had conversations with family back home to the tune of "never again in a kayak". They were immediately taking bets on how long it would be before my hat went back into the R2AK ring. Then, in a text conversation with Razzle Dazzle's Katy Stewart whilst waiting for that flight in Vancouver, the next team name came to me. When you have a team name, you're as good as committed.

Zen Again Dog?

You betcha.

References

This narrative is very much from the narrow perspective of the racer; my experience of Race to Alaska was blinkered by the visibility from my boat and my isolation from most of the rest of the competing fleet. I have included the passages written by Race Boss at Race to Alaska as I felt they counterbalanced my experience with an eloquent objectivity. It was quite something after the race to read outside-in accounts of what happened in the first hours of the race, and then of what transpired at Dungeness Lighthouse. I have included the latter, and highly recommend you seek out the former. As a seasoned tracker junkie with a love of those updates, I shouldn't have been surprised. As always with the daily updates, the turns of phrase, reverence, irreverence, and the eloquent use of American, makes you chuckle and inspires you at the same time. I'd encourage anyone who hasn't waded through the back catalogue of daily updates to do so.

The same goes for the team bio, also courtesy of the R2AK Race Boss. I have no idea what Prince Harry is really like. I'm sure he's a lovely bloke, and our paths have *nearly* crossed more than once in our lives, and to have him *and* the Harris tweed guy mentioned in the same article...? Again, I refer you to the R2AK website. The biographies are masterpieces.

The transcripts I've included of Dan Evans's monologues along the way just tickle me in that, at the time, I had no idea how off the grid I was. You cannot help but get swept up by Daniel's enthusiastic exhortations and his from-the-boat updates. I hope that their inclusion goes some way to conveying the near misses we had through the race. I did accidentally keep one step ahead of him, and I really wasn't going out of my way to keep a low profile. While I'd love to take credit for originating the "quaking ball of phlegm" when referring to COVID, I have to credit that to him also.

I wanted to include Rebecca Ross's field report because I found it to be an accurate, kind, and gentle telling of the last hours of my race in 2022. When I first read it, the article did make my eyes leak, and from what I can gather from friends back home who learned of my demise in the race by reading it, so did theirs too. I had no preconception of what the media would be like during my time on the water, and her and Lynette Oostmeyer were tolerant and very kind to an extremely miserable Brit on that last day.

The excerpt from Paula's article from the Peninsula Daily News shows how much of a good fist you can make of a fractured conversation with a Brit with no space or time to talk. I'm sorry Paula that I didn't make more time for your questions, but I enjoyed your write-up, and I'm especially glad you included the picture of the cakes.

I'm not going to reference all the planning materials I used. There are plenty of books and sites out there on the Inside Passage that do so comprehensively. However, there are one or two to single out. I did dog-ear the pages of Robert H. Miller's "Kayaking the Inside Passage", and I frequently returned to Denis Dwyer's books, scouring them for helpful nuggets, and there were plenty of those, not least his kit lists. I found Susan Conrad's "Inside" to be one of the most enjoyably readable accounts available. Start with these, and use their references, and you will almost certainly find the Inside Passage information that you're looking for.

Online, the BC Marine Trails maps proved invaluable, as did the Inside Passage Registry. The latter is a gateway to a veritable trove of accounts and information, and I spent weeks drifting through its contents. For any racer, the R2AK website itself is a diamond for anecdotes, and more importantly for using the old race tracker replays to work out where the campsites are, and most importantly what the optimum routes to follow are.

The eagle-eyed among you will have picked out the quotations beneath many of the chapter headings. I have always found the space race fascinating, and in shooting for my own moon in entering Race to Alaska, I found pieces of speeches and radio communication that complemented what was happening or how I felt during different points of the race. That, in training, I had Public Service Broadcasting's "The Race For Space" on repeat on my iPod and in the car, meant that Kennedy, Armstrong, Korolev et al were integral to my motivation. If you don't aim for the stars then you will never get there. Dream big. It is worth it.

Last, and maybe most, I am very grateful and privileged to have been allowed to borrow Edward Monkton's "Zen Dog" poem and adopt it for my team. I hope, Giles, that this story lives up to the canine spirit of your verse, and I did love being able to explain it to tracker junkies, journalists and anyone who would listen before, during, and after the race.

Acknowledgements

I would hope that, in writing this story, I have given credit to most of those along the way who made my experience of R2AK what it was. There are one or two who deserve singling out.

I am acutely aware that I have not mentioned my family. Without their patience, tolerance, and all manner of support, I could not have attempted this. Mum, Dad, Julie, James, and Mark: I know that I'm a bugger to live with when trips like these consume me. Thank you for putting up with me.

I had a lot of help preparing for this, especially from Richard, Max, Natasha, Jim, and Marieke for training, planning, and all-round support. Natasha, Rachel, Jen, Jo, Angela, and especially Mum, Dad, and Biz; you dug me out of a hole in 2020 and put me back on track when things went badly wrong. I cannot thank you enough for that.

Roger Chandler at Coastal Spirit: You set me on the right path and you never said "no", whatever doubts you may have harboured about my ability or sanity. If you want to learn to sea kayak, go with Roger. He's an awesome instructor.

Helen and Steve, along with Bill, were the rock of a pit crew that bookended my race and made the whole experience marginally less intimidating from a planning perspective. They also picked up a lot of pieces after this story ended, for which I am very grateful. Everyone should have a cousin like Old Bossy Boots.

In the immediate aftermath of my withdrawal, I had a lot of help as detailed above. Jamie, Bob, Shelley and Derrill, then Larry Roy, and especially the help through Lilian from David Linger was over and above any call of duty. I have not quite reconciled myself to being a complete dirtbag, but I felt nearer to Fred Beckey's lifestyle in those weeks in the States than I think I ever will again.

My race was about the kindness of strangers, and now I count those strangers as friends. Ian and Janice, Drew, Lilian, Liz, Diane, Patrick, and Peg; I am indebted to you for your help and the stories and memories we created.

And lastly Jake and Daniel. Our paths didn't cross as much as maybe they could have had my tracker worked, but your race is just a bit special, and thank you for letting me be a part of it.

Printed in Great Britain
by Amazon

35547494R00116